D1600313

# Sex, Then and Now

# Sex, Then and Now

Sexualities and the Bible

## William Loader

CASCADE *Books* · Eugene, Oregon

SEX, THEN AND NOW
Sexualities and the Bible

Cascade Books
An Imprint of Wipf and Stock Publishers
199 W. 8th Ave., Suite 3
Eugene, OR 97401

www.wipfandstock.com

PAPERBACK ISBN: 978-1-6667-0129-6
HARDCOVER ISBN: 978-1-6667-0130-2
EBOOK ISBN: 978-1-6667-0131-9

*Cataloguing-in-Publication data:*

Names: Loader, William R. G., 1944– [author].

Title: Sex, then and now : sexualities and the Bible / William Loader.

Description: Eugene, OR: Cascade Books, 2022 | Includes bibliographical references.

Identifiers: ISBN 978-1-6667-0129-6 (paperback) | ISBN 978-1-6667-0130-2 (hardcover) | ISBN 978-1-6667-0131-9 (ebook)

Subjects: LCSH: Sex—Biblical teaching | Bible and homosexuality | Marriage—Biblical teaching | Sex role—Biblical teaching | Sex—Religious aspects—Christianity | Same-sex marriage

Classification: BS680.S5 L63 2022 (print) | BS680.S5 (ebook)

04/15/22

# Contents

# Preface

THIS BOOK IS ABOUT sexualities. It is a book of listening. Listening to what biblical writers and others of their time, particularly Jewish authors, were writing, especially about sexual actions, attitudes, and orientations between people of the same gender. It is also a book about reflecting: on human experience and on what biblical authors wrote and why.

Listening, for me, means listening to the context in which people were expressing themselves. I have deliberately, therefore, ranged across a number of issues relating to sexuality and attitudes towards sexuality in these ancient texts and not limited myself to the very few that deal with sexual relations between people of the same gender. I have also not just written about such texts, but cited them directly, allowing their voices to be heard. I invite you to give yourself space and time to hear these ancient texts. I am aware that some will be unfamiliar, especially where I have cited Jewish authors from beyond the Hebrew Scriptures. They are worth hearing in themselves, but especially because they can give us some understanding of how, in turn, they heard biblical texts and interpreted them. Many of them were part of Paul's world and are important for understanding how Paul himself engaged such biblical texts.

Behind this book is also some listening to people in recent times, reading their reflections, observing their lives, watching them in public spaces and the media. I do not pretend, however, to be a specialist on contemporary theories and experiences of people now identified with the acronym, LGBTQ (Lesbian, Gay, Bisexual, Transgender, Queer). I have added 'I' (Intersex) when appropriate in the context.

Language can be contentious and confusing at times, not least in the discussion of sexualities. For some, sex means an action of sexual engagement. For others, the meaning of sex is wider but quite straightforward. It refers to biology and a person's genitalia. It has always seemed to me, however, that the most important sexual organ is the brain. One of the ways of seeking to avoid such confusions is to use the word "gender" and "gender identity," which can include how one's sees one's sexuality. Gender roles have often, of course, nothing to do with sexuality. My compromise in this book has been to prefer to use the language of gender as a more open term and allow the context of the discussion to define it.

Underlying this slim book is also a body of research in which I have been engaged, looking particularly at attitudes towards sexuality more broadly in early Jewish and Christian literature to the end of the first century CE. This research has been published in a number of works, listed at the conclusion of this book as "For Further Reading." These document in detail what is to be found in these ancient texts but also how they have been understood and are currently understood within the community of research. This book reflects, therefore, not only my own research but also the rich benefit of engaging the research of others to whom I remain ever grateful.

Unless otherwise indicated all biblical quotations are from the New Revised Standard Version. The sources for other works are cited in an Appendix.

While I take sole responsibility for all that I have written below, I want to acknowledge how valuable it has been to run the manuscript past colleagues and friends with diverse backgrounds and experiences and to receive their comments and feedback. I especially thank Elenie Poulos, Brandan Robertson, Alan Robinson, Betty Stroud, and, finally, my wife, Gisela Loader, who has accompanied me not just during the writing of this book but also for the past fifty-eight years.

William Loader

# Meet the Family!

Matters relating to diverse sexualities and gender identity have assumed growing significance in recent years. In some Christian circles they have taken center stage and become the focus of division, as have many other issues from time to time in the church from its very beginning.

LGBTQ is the acronym for people who are lesbian, gay, bisexual, transgender, and queer. People who identify themselves by such descriptors may be attracted to people of the same gender (lesbian or gay) or to people of different genders. This book addresses sexualities among people of the same gender in a very broad sense and, while focusing on ancient texts, does so with an awareness that human experience is diverse and needs to inform what we hear and what we think.

I want to begin with some listening. It is not possible nor appropriate for me to publish a transcript of a family discussion, so I have composed the following as what might be typical experiences of many as a way of introducing the topic. I invite your indulgence and your imagination to listen in.

ᴄᴏ ᴄᴏ

Helen sat stirring her coffee, dissolving the neat image created by the barista. "That's how I feel," she mused out loud. "I'm now confused. It used to be clear, just as June said." She was referring back to the discussion group she and her friends, Brian and Jill, had just left together.

June had stated in no uncertain terms: "It's an abomination. The Bible says. It's sin. It was sin then and it's sin now."

Jason, another member of the group, was just as forthright: "Get a life, June. How can it be sin? Some people are straight, and some people are gay. Everyone knows that. How can it be sin to be what you are?"

"Well then, if you're gay you should not act it out. You should get help. Let God heal you and make you right," June insisted.

Brian didn't want to talk about it. Inside he was churning.

Jill echoed Helen's thoughts of confusion, but for Helen the situation was a bit more real and personal because of her brother, Kevin. And the situation with Kevin was not an issue only for her, but was also troubling her parents.

Her parents, Evelyn and John, like many in their generation, were taken by surprise by Kevin. What seemed just a close relation between Kevin and Geoff as just good buddies became a problem when one day John saw them being very physically affectionate.

Evelyn didn't think there was a problem. They were both very proud of Kevin and had seen his friendship with Geoff very positively. "They're always together," said Evelyn. "I think it's great. They help each other in their studies. They do things together, play sport together. I think it's wonderful." Evelyn was in no doubt.

"He's a lucky boy," her husband, John, added. "When I was fourteen, I was quite lonely. It was hard to make friends. And then, of course, there were girls and what did you do?"

"He's not into that, yet. Give it time. I'm sure he'll find a girl-friend. There's no sense in hurrying things." Evelyn sighed: "He's not going to put us through the troubles we had with Helen."

Helen, Kevin's elder sister, four years older, had kept John and Evelyn on their toes. First child, of course, and a new world of growing up and anxious parents. But she turned out alright, even though she didn't always keep good company.

John was still not quite sure. Then one Sunday they were sharing morning tea with their pastor after church, while their children were engaged in youth group activities.

"Geoff and Kevin are very close, aren't they?" the pastor remarked.

"Yes, great friends," said Evelyn.

And then John added. "They really are very close and sometimes I find it a bit strange. They hug each other for a long time and . . ."—he stopped going further.

The pastor listened with a perceptive ear. "Don't worry," he said. "Kids of that age go through phases. It's part of adolescence. Their emotions are sometimes all over the place."

"Do you think it's just an adolescent phase?" Evelyn remarked, when she and John were relaxing for the evening. The pastor had set her thinking. "He's always played mainly with boys. That's just the way he is."

Time passed and little changed. Both Kevin and Geoff were in the youth group. They seemed to spend endless time on their iPhones and iPads, sometimes well into the night. Then John was watching one day when Geoff dropped in and again there was a long hug that seemed very affectionate and loving. This time he reported this to Evelyn. "Do you think everything is okay?" They were clearly being very loving towards each other each time they met. That became the norm. John and Evelyn would notice and then say, "Well, that's how they are."

Some months later they were again with the pastor at morning tea after church and he again asked how Kevin was doing. John reported how Kevin and Geoff were physically very affectionate. The pastor listened carefully and then in the gentlest way said: "I think you need to watch what's happening. Something could be going wrong. This is how kids get into same-gender sexual relations and go down a path that leads to serious wrongdoing. God made men and women to be together. Men getting together with men and women getting together with women—I mean sexually—is an

3

abomination, a perversion of how God made us to be. I would try to encourage Kevin not to spend so much time with Geoff or this could go badly wrong."

That comment was quite a shock and set John and Evelyn back on their heels. Later John said, "Have we been harboring sin without knowing it?"

"Let's take it carefully," responded Evelyn. "He's a good boy. He's not evil. He probably doesn't realize the dangers."

So they took to persuading Kevin not to go round to Geoff's place so much and not to spend so much time with him. In a move that seemed quite opposite to how they handled their daughter, they began to encourage Kevin to think about girls. How far would they go? Certainly not putting pornography before him, but at least talking up female attractiveness. Evelyn made a first move by suggesting to Kevin, "Why don't you ask Carol to go out on a date with you?" Carol was one of the youth group.

They also invited youth group members into their home, especially the young attractive girls. They even succeeded, eventually, in persuading Kevin to pluck up courage and invite Carol to the movies. When he came home, they were still up and were dying to ask how it went and what he felt but were careful to hold back. Kevin went out with Carol a few times.

One night John heard Kevin still awake and talking. Privacy is important so he didn't want to be nosey, but it happened so often that one day he tried listening at the door. Was he talking to Carol? No. He was talking to Geoff. He was talking to Geoff about Carol. Something else began to happen. Instead of inviting Geoff to come around or going round to his place, Kevin would just go out jogging. Going out jogging was a way he could meet up with Geoff in the park. He knew his parents wouldn't approve, so always felt slightly guilty because he loved his mum and dad, but he also loved Geoff.

Girlfriends? There was Carol and then Christine and then Andrea. They came and went, but there was always Geoff. John and Evelyn figured out what was happening. They had just driven Kevin and Geoff into secrecy. "What have we done?" mused John one evening. "Where did we go wrong? Did I spend too much time with him when he was a baby when you were having a down?"

"I don't think we went wrong," said Evelyn. "This is just the way he is. Remember? Even as a preschooler. It's like he was born that way. It's in his genes."

It worried John so much that he had begun researching. "No, there's no gay gene," he said. "I think we have seen it as something that can just go wrong in some people, like having a disability, but it really is a serious condition. I talked to our pastor the other day and he said that the whole thing is about sin, Adam's sin. That's when things started going wrong and what we have to do is work against it. It is a perversion of how God made us. The Bible condemns it as an abomination and a perversion, not just the acts that might follow, but also the orientation itself. He suggested we talk to Kevin and see if he would agree to undergo what they call 'conversion therapy,' a way of blocking gay feelings and turning them to become heterosexual feelings. Jesus can save him from this state of sin and we should now be acting as God's agents to restore Kevin back to what is natural."

"Wow. That's a lot to digest," said Evelyn. I don't think he's bad or a sinner, but it sure is unnatural and I can see that unless we do something, we will be complicit in encouraging our son down a path to perversion. We love Kevin, so we have to do something."

"We need to be firm," added John. "We don't want to be responsible for letting our son get into this. I sometimes have these horrible dreams of seeing him marching in gay parades or seeing him cowering and condemned before God, destined for hell."

"It's a real worry," reflected Evelyn. "But I find it hard to think it's all so bad. Think of Uncle Andrew and his friend we call Uncle Rex. They live together. As kids we always found it strange that they slept in the same bed. I think they still do. And then there was Mrs. Perkins. She and Miss Sampson did the same, so someone said. They were always together. Nobody seemed to bother. Perhaps they did and we never knew. They were all good people as far as I know. Uncle Rex used to play the organ at church."

"Those were times when people didn't twig to what was happening," John replied. "And those who were identified as 'homos' out in the open—remember: poofters, gays, queers—were widely despised and their acts deemed criminal. To be like that was to choose to be an outcast. You deserved society's condemnation. With lesbians, like Mrs. Perkins, it wasn't so bad, because you could imagine that they couldn't get up to too much, but the others were seriously bad people and many of them preyed on kids, even some brothers and priests in church institutions. All such people stood under God's judgement."

"It must have been terrible for them," Evelyn responded, "because some of them were good people, like Kevin. Imagine being treated like you're a pervert and pedophile when you're really just a person with an unnatural orientation. Kevin's not like that. I'd hate to see him hated and categorized like that. He's our son. We love him. But perhaps the pastor's right. Now is the time to act. I have, however, been doing a bit of my own reading and there's a seminary professor who's been saying that we've got it all wrong about the Bible. It doesn't condemn gays at all but is only talking about people being excessive or engaging in pedophilia or male prostitution in pagan temples. I suspect that this may be just trying to explain away what seems very plain to me, as our pastor said. I would, however, like to know more. I'd hate us to do anything that might harm or hurt Kevin one way or other. I want to be sure we're doing the right thing and I suspect we're not alone. It would be terrible if we got it wrong."

Helen was aware that her mum and dad were troubled about Kevin, but when she spoke with Kevin, he didn't see himself as a problem at all. It was a little different with Geoff, his friend. He was sometimes happy and sometimes very unhappy. "Sometimes he cries, and I don't know what to do," Kevin said. He trusted his sister, Helen, and knew he could confide in her. He also knew Jason and they sometimes talked. Geoff's family wasn't happy at all. That was hard for him and that made his relationship with Kevin all the more important. In some ways Kevin was his lifeline.

သာ ၹာ

There are many other stories to tell and many that you could tell, I am sure. Some of them are painful and full of prejudice and hurt. Some of them leave you wondering.

There is the woman married for forty years, now widowed, and finding closeness with another widowed woman: forming a pair, living together, loving one another. Are they lesbian? It hardly matters to define what is happening. Is it just a sexual component that would warrant that label? They would see that as absurd. There is so much more to their relationship—but that is how they would label themselves now if pressed.

I have respect and awe for senior leaders in society and the church who have identified themselves as lesbian, gay, or queer, long after they have become known and highly regarded for their moral leadership. They are anything but rebels. But how did people respond? In the eyes of some, it seriously diminished the good reputations that had been built over years. For others, it has brought a confusion of voices, their own sometimes telling them that these are good people and sometimes telling them that they are an abomination; they must be sinners. Yet for others, the presence and impact of openly gay role models is more effective than intellectual arguments for persuading them that some people simply are that way and that it is okay.

Or what about the adolescent boy who found himself in love with another boy in his class, wrote poems to express his affection, even delighted in holding his hand or hugging him, but then ever since has always had attraction to the opposite gender and never again to someone of his own gender? It wasn't a wild fling, but was it a temporary descent into sin? Did he even think about it? It all happened at a time when the issue was not on the public agenda and LGBTQ people were hidden in fear in their communities, and he realized only years later that he had had a homoerotic experience, something about which he had no idea. He was a committed believer, a teenage evangelist, no less. How would other people have reacted and what would he have done in an era of awareness like ours? Been overwhelmed with guilt and confessed his sin? Felt pressured to nail his colors to the mast and declare that for then and ever he was gay?

Maybe we know someone whose life collapsed into a spiral of guilt and self-loathing about their own sexual orientation or gender identity, leading to a tragic end. "I can't help it. I am an abomination. I don't know what to do. I know what they think. I don't know what I think. This has to end"—and sadly that end is sometimes sought in the loneliness of death. And so many have been in and out of that valley of dread. Voices of hope call to them. "Believe, trust! Let Christ heal you!" They embark, strongly motivated by the encouragement of those around them and by their own convictions, on a course of so-called conversion "therapy," to make themselves "normal" again. They expose themselves to negative vibes in response to same-gender sexual feelings; reward themselves with positive vibes and rewards for keeping God's commandments. Add lots of love and compassion in the process, and they have high hopes to be set right.

I know only of those who have tried this and failed. Some jurisdictions ban such conversion practices. Are they putting a block in the way of full salvation? I know of others who, abandoning such notions of "normality," have come to accept the way they are, which they now see as not sinful, but as their normality. Then in response to what they read as the prohibitions of Scripture they commit themselves to celibacy, not acting out their passions, at least not in a way that would lead to genital engagement with others. They seek to channel their sexual energies elsewhere and sometimes, in the process, give birth to art and other forms of creativity. For some, this appears to work. For others, it does not. And, at best, those for whom it does work do not seek to impose it on others or imply it should be the norm.

And what of those who knew they were gay or lesbian and chose to marry heterosexual partners whom they also loved, in the hope that this would in time refocus their desires and orientation? Did it work? Many stayed with the commitment. Others found no lasting fulfilment and had to grapple with guilt, anger, disappointment, and not knowing where to turn.

And let us not overlook others whose rebellious spirit expresses itself in wild sexual adventures, flaunting their profligacy, affronting the norms, sometimes as just one aspect of a repertoire of behaviors designed to give the finger, as it were, to all authority, including God. Often, they are fueled by drugs and alcohol. Such rebelliousness is, however, not gendered. It occurs across the broad spectrum of society, gay, straight, and bi, and to suggest otherwise is simply prejudice. Where such prejudice is rife, there is room for protest and also for positive celebration of difference.

Another area where prejudice often emerges is where people speak as if pedophilia is the special reserve of gay men (and sometimes gay women). But this is absurd, ignoring both the fact that the vast majority of gay people are not pedophiles but also the fact that many pedophiles are heterosexual and their victims often not limited to one gender. Such abuse, too often hidden by institutions concerned to correct and rebuke but not expose, has come to light in unexpected places. Such crimes, when involving same-gender abuse, have fed the prejudice that gay men are perverts and predatory monsters and has held in place the dangerous hate that damned them all and all too often expressed itself and alas still does in gay bashings.

So, what is abominable? What is abusive? What is sin? What are sinful acts? What are sinful attitudes? What is unnatural? What is natural? Is what makes certain heterosexual behaviors sin also what makes certain gay behaviors sin? Is homosexual orientation itself sinful?

How can we differentiate? Some things are obvious, so obvious and uncontroversial that they are defined as criminal acts: rape, abuse, sexual violence, exploitation, pedophilia. Some are yet to be enshrined in law, such as coercive control, or may never be. Most people, regardless of their sexual orientation and gender identity, are not engaged in such criminal activity. They, not least those who embrace the message of love at the heart of the gospel, seek to live productive and fulfilling lives, which at their best are informed by values of respect and love.

It is when we move beyond the obviously illegal and forbidden to the wide range of attitudes and behaviors expressed by people who see themselves as "normal" and law-abiding that issues arise that need addressing, not least in relation to being gay. In many jurisdictions, being gay is now no longer criminalized and LBGTQI+ people have been afforded protections in law from prejudice and discrimination, and in many countries same-gender marriage has been legalized. It's now widely considered quite OK to be gay. There are other countries, however, where homosexuality is punishable by imprisonment or even death.

Where does this leave someone who seeks to live responsibly and be a follower of Jesus nourished by the Scriptures? Never mind what legislatures say: what does *the Bible* say and how can we take it seriously in the light of our faith and our life experience?

This book provides an account of what the Bible says, or more specifically what the biblical writers were saying and the meaning of what they said when interpreted in the context of their thought and the world of their day. I have written it on the basis of having undertaken detailed research on attitudes towards sexuality in early Jewish writings and early Christian writing to the end of the first century BCE. The "Further Reading" section at the end of this book lists these works. I seek to be as clear as possible about what people said and meant *then* and not to try to reframe it to suit my or anyone else's point of view. It is for this reason that my research has been used as a resource by people arguing quite opposite points of view about how we should respond to what biblical writers were saying.

It is my belief that current discussions are best served by our being as accurate as possible about the biblical material. My own stance sees a need for us, with our modern understanding of the world, sometimes to approach the issues differently from the way biblical writers mostly did, based on their ancient understandings of reality. However, I believe that this first requires being strict and honest about what is there in the texts, and that is what I seek to do. Then let people make up their own minds.

Our exploration will begin with the so-called Old Testament, the Hebrew Scriptures. It will include looking at the creation stories in Genesis, the prohibitions in Leviticus, and a number of other texts in which people have found allusions to issues of same-gender sexuality. We then move to other Jewish writings, mostly from later times, both to see what they say and to hear how they interpreted what biblical writers wrote. We shall also look at what was being said in the wider Greco-Roman world before turning to the New Testament itself, in particular to the writings of Paul, who had most to say on the topic. The concluding chapter will return to our "family," to explore options that people have taken in the light of the biblical material and contemporary experience and observation.

# 2

# The Old Testament

THIS CHAPTER HAS FOUR main parts. In the first we turn to the stories of creation, which were and remain so influential in shaping people's understandings of sexuality. Then we look at the many stories and themes that deal with sexual matters, especially those reflecting the norms that governed households and how household members should behave. That then leads, in the third part, to a set of specific prohibitions among which there are two dealing with sexual acts between men. We conclude by looking at a series of stories that have been read as possibly having relevant content.

## Creation

"In the beginning God created the heaven and the earth." These are the first words of the Bible in the Bible of my youth, the Authorized King James Version. Next to them in my Bible in the left-hand margin was a date: "4004 BC." The date is based on a calculation by Archbishop James Ussher, Anglican primate of all Ireland, 1625–26, which included adding up the dates in genealogies of Old Testament figures. He was even more precise: creation began on 23 October, 4004 BCE.

You might reach, at least, a similar year if you did the adding up yourself. It would not be unreasonable if you assumed that all dates preserving people's age in the Bible were accurate. That would include Methuselah who, according to Gen 5:27, lived for 969 years. Make that just ninety-six instead and you have creation dated to 3008 BCE. The universe as we know it is considerably older than that, to say the least, usually reckoned to be 13.5 billion years old!

"So," declare some, "the Bible can't be trusted because it is clearly wrong!" Not so fast! You can't dismiss the Bible just like that. Of course, it is wrong. The authors of Genesis had knowledge limited to the science of their times. What else should one expect? Just because we find in this collection of Israel's ancient traditions a source of inspiration and challenge, indeed claim to hear God addressing us through them, does not mean that they are other than human, always preserving absolutely accurate scientific information. Rather, they bear all the traits of being human. Those who simply say "The Bible is the Word of God" and mean by that that it records God's words, and so must be absolutely true in every respect, are committing themselves to defend the impossible.

The alternative is not to dismiss the Bible but to understand that as a source of inspiration and challenge it comes to us with all the usual trappings one would expect of a writing or collection of writings from an ancient culture, reflecting the world of its time. People in recent centuries have come to read the Bible in ways that do it greater justice, taking it more seriously. That means making an effort to listen more carefully, including by reading it in its own languages, Hebrew for the Old, Greek for the New. That greater care has also meant taking it more seriously as a collection of writings that reflect very specific historical and cultural contexts and make use of a range of different forms of writing, genres. Some of its writings read more like history annals, at least in form. Others are clearly poetry. Some are collections of rules and commandments. Some are stories, such as we find in surrounding cultures, told to explain why things are the way they are in nature and society.

The stories in the first chapters of the Book of Genesis belong to the category of such stories. We can be tempted to dismiss them as mere stories or myths or we can treat them as gospel truth. Neither approach, however, does them justice. We need to make an effort to hear not only their storylines but also the *meaning* those stories are seeking to convey. The story of the building of the Tower of Babel is a good example. It tells how "the whole earth had one language and the same words" (Gen 11:1) and how people built a high tower, saying, "Come, let us build ourselves a city, and a tower with its top in the heavens, and let us make a name for ourselves" (11:4). According to the story, God's response was to say:

> "Come, let us go down, and confuse their language there, so that they will not understand one another's speech." So the LORD scattered them abroad from there over the face of all the earth, and they left off building the city. Therefore it was called Babel, because there the LORD confused the language of all the earth; and from there the LORD scattered them abroad over the face of all the earth. (Gen 11:7–9)

The story probably had its origins beyond Israel. The "Let *us* go down," sounds like the echo of an older story underlying the present one in which multiple gods were involved and not just God, though that may not be the case. Furthermore, we know that language development was much more complex than this story suggests, developing over tens of thousands of years. Be that as it may, consider the *meaning* of the story: for we also know that when people try to make a name for themselves, communication often breaks down. And that is a valuable insight of perennial relevance central to the meaning of the story.

When we turn to the creation stories, in particular the creation of man and woman, we see signs that the wisdom of storytellers has been at work there, too. Creation over seven days matched the seven-day week of daily life, including the seventh day as a day of rest. To read this as literally and scientifically correct is deeply problematic at multiple levels, not least at the level of the text itself. Days, as skeptics used to point out with glee, cannot exist until the sun is made and yet it comes into being only on day four! Some of those who struggle to hold onto the story as accurate science while recognizing the problem with seven literal days of creation try to explain away the days as seven long periods of time, but this is to overlook the remaining problems (such as light and plants appearing before the sun) and is to misread the nature of these writings just as much as the hardline fundamentalist. However, there is no need for skepticism and glee at the folly of believers; just a need for cross-cultural sensitivity to understand what this ancient culture was saying. Ultimately, it is that God created the world and what God created is good.

There is some indication that the writers of Genesis were gathering stories of origin, because in fact they include two accounts of creation. The first has human beings created on the sixth day as the pinnacle of creation, after the animals, the plants, under the sky as a dome (Gen 1:26–28). The second begins with the creation of a human being, made first as a clay model and then breathed into life by God (Gen 2:7), and recounts how God made a garden and then created the animals as companions for the man and finally made woman as the most suitable companion. Thus, it begins:

> In the day that the LORD God made the earth and the heavens, when no plant of the field was yet in the earth and no herb of the field had yet sprung up—for the LORD God had not caused it to rain upon the earth, and there was no one to till the ground; but a stream would rise from the earth, and water the whole face of the ground— then the LORD God formed man from the dust of the ground, and breathed into his nostrils the breath of life; and the man became a living being. (Gen 2:4–7)

The writers quite happily included the two accounts because they could combine them to reflect on the wonders of God's creation. Only a dilettante would complain that the sequence is wrong: plants and animals came before humans, surely! The writers were focusing on human beings and on how and why they were created and so discrepancies over when plants and animals were created did not matter. These were significant stories, not historical reports. From their perspective, the two accounts fitted well together.

The creation of humans necessarily included reference to sexuality and gender. In the first creation story we read that God created humankind. All creation is by divine initiative, but creating humankind is singled out for special mention:

> Then God said, "Let us make humankind in our image, according to our likeness; and let them have dominion over the fish of the sea, and over the birds of the air, and over the cattle, and over all the wild animals of the earth, and over every creeping thing that creeps upon the earth." (Gen 1:26)

Accordingly, it is done:

> So God created humankind in his image, in the image of God he created them; male and female he created them. God blessed them, and God said to them, "Be fruitful and multiply, and fill the earth and subdue it and have dominion over the fish of the sea and over the birds of the air and over every living thing that moves upon the earth." (Gen 1:27–28)

The "image" and "likeness" is not that humans looked like God in appearance, nor that God was male and female, but that humans were to exercise oversight and control over creation as God does. More importantly, God made humankind male and female, men and women. As such they were to be fruitful and multiply. They should have sexual intercourse and reproduce. God had given similar instruction to the fish and birds: "God blessed them, saying, 'Be fruitful and multiply and fill the waters in the seas, and let birds multiply on the earth'" (1:22) and the same is the assumed mandate for the animals, made the next day.

There can be no doubt: God made human beings (and the others) as sexual beings and did so for the purpose of reproduction. God made sex and sex is a good thing. That was important for people to know. Sex is for making offspring.

By adding the second account of creation the writers supplemented this insight and understanding of human sexuality. They read the second account as explaining *how* God created male and female. The word "humankind" in Gen 1:27 is the Hebrew word *'adam*. Read in the light of the second creation story, the human made in 1:27 is a man, a male. The Hebrew word *'adam* is then treated as his name: Adam. Adam was, accordingly, the first human being and was male. They read the account of his creation in Gen 1:27 not as saying that he was male and female, but that he was male. The text, which I translate literally, makes that clear: "God created humankind (*'adam*) in his image, in the image of God he created him; male and female he created them." It does not say: Male and female he created *him*. They read generic term *'adam* as referring to a male human being, as the story in chapter 2 assumes.

Thus, the writers filled out the meaning of "male and female he created them" through the second creation story. It begins with a man, Adam, and reports how God sought companions for him: "It is not good that the man should be alone; I will make him a helper as his partner" (2:18), and so created animals. That did not fulfil his need: "For the man there was not found a helper as his partner" (2:20). At this point God engages in a new act of creation:

> So the LORD God caused a deep sleep to fall upon the man, and he slept; then he took one of his ribs and closed up its place with flesh. And the rib that the LORD God had taken from the man he made into a woman and brought her to the man. Then the man said, "This at last is bone of my bones and flesh of my flesh; this one shall be called Woman, for out of Man this one was taken." Therefore a man leaves his father and his mother and clings to his wife, and they become one flesh. (Gen 2:21–24)

Greek legend told of the creation of woman as an act of anger on the part of Zeus, who, confronted by arrogant and disrespectful humans, some of whom had both male and female genitalia, sliced them in half, resulting in some who were male and some who were female. Ever since they have tried to re-join. The story in Genesis is at one level similar but at another very different. Creating woman was not an act of anger but one of favor and generosity. The result is similar: they will seek to re-join, which is seen in Genesis as something very positive.

While this ancient theory of the origins of sexual desire belongs to the past in the history of ideas, its claim that God created sex and affirmed sexual intercourse remains its lasting value. Indeed, "clings to" is a word meaning "having sexual intercourse with" and the "one flesh" is about oneness and intimacy. Sexual intercourse and sexual engagement are part of what God made possible in response to seeing the need for the man to have companionship.

Two roles for sexual intercourse and sexual engagement emerge from these accounts of creation. The first is human reproduction. The second is companionship and a sense of oneness, intimacy. This, of course, finds its celebration in the Song of Songs. Both roles would be connected in the ancient world, indeed in the pre-contraceptive world right up until recent decades. For, in real-life experience, sexual intimacy in oneness and human reproduction belonged together. Even then, however, the two did not necessarily always go together and only a narrow rigorist misreading of the texts would insist that there can be no sexual intimacy if not for reproduction, requiring abstention, for instance, during pregnancy or menstruation or after menopause.

The creation stories reflect on common experience, explaining, as such stories did, why things are the way they are. They also provide the basis for reflection on marriage as the way in which the man and the woman are to become one flesh, one kin, and so create family. English enables us to reproduce the pun, present in the Hebrew, when it declares: "this one shall be called *ishshah* (woman), for out of *ish* (man) this one was taken" (Gen 2:23). Hebrew writers were fond of playing with words in this way. For instance, they explain that '*adam* was taken from the dust of the ground ('*adamah*) (2:7). Similarly, the fact that the word for "breath" was also the word for "wind" and "spirit" made for many helpful plays on words, such as the statement that God breathed into the clay model of the human and it came to life (Gen 2:7) and that God's spirit/breath/wind was blowing/moving across the face of the waters at the beginning of creation (Gen 1:2).

Word plays continue as the account which follows the creation of woman indicates that "the man and his wife were both naked ('*arumim*), and were not ashamed" (Gen 2:25) and then goes on to write of the snake as "cunning" ('*arum*) (Gen 3:1). Nakedness became problematic after Eve and Adam fell for the snake's cunning and so the story explains for its world why people wear clothes.

Their sin served to explain also so much more: why humans no longer live in paradisal conditions, why women have pain in giving birth, why they keep coming back to their husbands and getting pregnant, why husbands rule over wives, why men have to work so hard, why thorns and thistles grow, and why people die (Gen 3:16–19). Such explanations, of course, need a thorough revision and make little sense in the light of today's knowledge, but the wisdom of the storyteller endures: cross forbidden boundaries and there are serious consequences. Humans who overreach and refuse to face their limitations bring serious harm on others and on themselves. Sin matters, and has consequences far beyond the immediate.

Sex has a role among these consequences as depicted in Genesis 3:16, with the suggestion that women will be (overly) desirous of their husbands and so keep falling pregnant. The translation of the Hebrew into Greek, the version of the Bible that informed Christian beginnings, added some elements not in the original, largely through ambiguity.

The translators formulated God's reflection about making women in a way that more closely matched the creation of the man in 1:26. Instead of having God say, "I will make" in 2:19 as in the Hebrew original, the translation reads, "Let us make," which matches "Let us make" in 1:26. The Greek also uses a word for "like" in "helper *like* him" which echoes the word used in 1:26 for "likeness" in "according to our likeness." This led many to read the Greek text as implying: as man was made in the image of God, so woman was made in the image of man. They saw it implying a hierarchy. God, then men, then women, in that order of superiority.

We find Paul doing so when, in his letter to the Corinthians, he writes: "For a man ought not to have his head veiled, since he is the image and reflection of God; but woman is the reflection of man" (1 Cor 11:7).

Similarly, Eve's explanation of her sin, namely that the snake tricked her (Gen 3:13), comes into Greek with a word that not only means tricked but also "seduced." This was not a meaning of the Hebrew word. Accordingly, people could read Gen 3:13 as stating that she was seduced. Again, Paul does so in 2 Cor 11:2–3, where he writes: "I feel a divine jealousy for you, for I promised you in marriage to one husband, to present you as a chaste virgin to Christ. But I am afraid that as the serpent deceived [literally: seduced] Eve by its cunning, your thoughts will be led astray from a sincere and pure devotion to Christ." Clearly, sexual seduction is meant, which would mean they would no longer be a chaste virgin. This kind of reading of Gen 3:13 fitted the widespread prejudice that women were less able to control their sexuality and thus more easily seduced and more readily seductive. The prejudice owes its origin in part to the practice of men in their world usually marrying women around half their age and misreading their inexperience and incapacity.

Where is there reference to same-gender orientation in the Genesis creation stories? Nowhere. It was obvious to them then, and many since, that there were only two types of human beings—just look at their bodies, they argue! They are male or female. No in-betweens, let alone people outwardly one thing and inwardly another. God made humankind male and female, and he made them heterosexual: as put popularly: "God made Adam and Eve not Adam and Steve." To those who suggest that this simple binary definition is not adequate, they respond, show me the biblical evidence! There is none, they declare. Gen 1:27 is enough and we should take it seriously.

For others, the statement needs to be read in the context of what these stories really are. That is, it needs to be weighed along with all the other explanations in the light of all that we know and experience. Is declaring humankind male and female an idea that endures in the light of what we now know from the sciences? Is it like the abiding insights from the story of Adam and Eve, namely, that sin is overreach? Or from the story of the tower of Babel, that making a name for oneself is a recipe for communication breakdown? Or from the creation stories, that God is good and creation in good? Or, rather, does it belong with the statements implied or expressed about the age of creation, about making a human from a clay model or a woman from a man's rib, or about the origins of painful contractions and death?

A sensitive cross-cultural reading, appropriate to the nature of these writings, requires that we give them the respect of taking what they say seriously and engaging it with integrity in the light of what we have so far learned about reality. My own assessment is that it no longer makes sense to treat male and female as an abiding and exclusive definition of the nature of human beings and their sexual identity. While most people fall into the category of male or female, some do not, not least those born intersex, that is, with sexual or reproductive anatomy that does not match the typical definitions of male and female, and those whose inner gender orientation does not reflect their anatomy.

## From Patriarchs to Prohibition: Sex and the Household

The creation stories of Genesis come at the beginning of the Bible. More specifically, they come at the beginning of the collection of five writings, sometimes called the Books of Moses: Genesis, Exodus, Leviticus, Numbers, and Deuteronomy. It is in Leviticus that we find the prohibitions usually cited in relation to gay matters. They are part of this wider collection of stories and regulations from early Israel. Before turning to them specifically we need to hear them within the context of this collection and hear what else it says beyond what we considered in the first few chapters of Genesis.

The collection took its final form at the hands of learned priests in the sixth or perhaps fifth century. They brought together much older material, including stories going back to tales of Israel's tribal ancestors, and their journeys and adventures, including the story of their entry into, and then exit from, Egypt. Sometimes there are traces of collections of various origins within this material which, over time, were brought together into the present work.

We can often trace more than one version of a story because it will have featured in different collections. For instance, the same person, Moses' father-in-law, is called Jethro in one version and Reuel in another. Sometimes we can even see that one collection preferred to call God Yahweh, and another preferred the word Elohim (usually simply translated by the word "God"). It seems that the Book of Deuteronomy was part of an even wider collection that also included later writings like Judges and the books of Samuel and Kings. Learned priestly circles will have brought all this material together. Sometimes we can detect their particular style and interests, not least in bodies of laws and regulations, which show signs of having been revised and updated over time.

In this rich collection, sexual themes are far from absent. In the broadest sense, they are present in the stories of the patriarchs, Abraham, Isaac, and Jacob. Both Abraham and Jacob had more than one wife and in addition slept with their slaves. Polygyny, having more than one wife, was considered normal and acceptable, as was having slaves, and even Josephus, the Jewish historian writing in the late first century CE, defends polygyny, though by his time monogamy, having just one wife (or one husband), the usual pattern in Hellenistic and Roman culture, had become the norm.

The norm for households was that the man was the head of the household and so had sexual access to all women within his household, with the exception of where it would constitute incest. While we may assume, rightly or wrongly, that consent mostly played a role with wives, this was less likely with slaves, so that behind the stories we read are hidden stories of sexual abuse and rape. Theirs was not a world where two young people fell in love and resolved to marry. Fathers arranged marriages, with or without their children's consent, especially their daughters' consent, because marriages were crucial for households and *households were crucial for economic survival* and so could not be left to romantic whims. Marriage was thus *everyone's* business, not just that of the couple. The household was the basis of the economy. Through craft and agriculture, it was the main source of financial support and also the main source of welfare support for the young, the aged, and the sick.

It was in the interest of the extended family, therefore, that people also married within the family, not outside it. Hence Abraham's sending his slave to accompany Isaac on a journey to find Rebecca, Isaac's cousin (Genesis 24). Rebecca herself, was, in turn, appalled that her son, Esau, married two Canaanite women. These were not only outside the family but foreigners (Gen 26:34–35; 27:46; 28:6–9).

Concern about intermarriage with foreign nations featured in later stories. Phinehas became famous for his zeal in spearing an Israelite man and his Midianite wife, a foreigner, for engaging in a mixed marriage (Num 25:1–9). Ezra and Nehemiah strongly oppose mixed marriages (Ezra 9:1–2; Neh 10:28–30). There was also, however, a counter current. Joseph had married Asenath, an Egyptian (Gen 41:45); Moses married Zipporah, a Midianite (Exod 2:21); Boaz married Ruth, a Moabite (Ruth 4:10); and Esther married a foreign king. Not all such marriages reflected well on their heroes. David shamefully abducted Bathsheba, presumably a foreigner, and also arranged for her husband, Uriah the Hittite, to be killed so that he, David, could marry her (2 Samuel 11). Solomon's excesses, including foreign wives, gave the lie to the view of many that he was wise (1 Kgs 11:1–2).

Judah, Jacob's son, married Shua, a foreign woman, also seen as unacceptable (Genesis 38). Disaster followed. His first son, Er, described as evil, married Tamar, also a foreigner. When he died, Judah told his second son, Onan, to sleep with her and produce offspring, but he refused, ejaculating his semen outside her vagina during sex. (Later Onanism became a term for masturbation.)

Things went from bad to worse when Judah then told Tamar to remain a widow, but then fell for her trap and slept with her himself, when she dressed herself as a prostitute and tricked him. Her offspring, the fruit of Judah's sleeping with her, were the forbears of David's royal line. The story depicts Judah's sin, not as his visiting a prostitute, but as his unwitting act of incest, sleeping with his son's wife. In an age where men married around thirty a woman around half that age, prostitution had an especially ready market among unmarried men. It featured from time to time in stories. Sometimes prostitutes were heroes, such as Rahab, who hid the spies in Jericho, and so prostitutes were not always condemned, as later became the norm. Later generations praised Tamar because she at least prioritized sleeping with her Israelite father-in-law, Judah, and perpetuated his line instead of marrying an Egyptian. Incest was the lesser of two evils, as the author of the first-century CE Pseudo-Philo pointed out (LAB 9:5).

Strict rules governed marriage, not least the prohibition of adultery. This, again, was not primarily for the hurt that one partner might cause the other but because breakdown of the marriage threatened the security of the household and everyone in it. This was to a large degree because contraception was rarely available or effective and illegitimate offspring might bring outsider control where it had no place. Israel's laws required the death penalty for both involved in adultery (Exod 20:14; Deut 5:18). Later, when under the Romans the right to execute was withdrawn, they had to conform to the rule in Roman culture, where divorce was compulsory when adultery had taken place—no counselling, no reconciliation. Theirs was a very different world.

Closely related to such rules is the law prohibiting the return of a woman to her husband once he had divorced her, especially if she had married another and then wanted to return (Deut 24:1–4). Adultery was not a ground for divorce in older times, as we have seen, because the law required that adulterers be sentenced to death. There were other grounds for divorce, however, and these were largely at the whim of the man. These matters were talked about from a male point of view. The underlying rule was that if you divorced your wife and she married and so slept with another man, she became unclean and forbidden to you, even if you wanted to have her back if her second marriage failed.

That rule applied also when Reuben, Jacob's eldest son, slept with Jacob's slave, Bilhah (Gen 35:22). Jacob could never sleep with her again. The story of Pharaoh abducting Sarah, Abraham's wife, believing Abraham's lie that she was his sister (Gen 12:10–20), caused great anxiety among those who retold the story. Why? Because if Pharaoh had slept with her, Sarah would have been forbidden to return to Abraham when his lie was found out. Those who retold the story often went to great lengths to say that Pharaoh did not do so—because the time was short or because he fell ill! To hurt his father, Absalom had sex with David's female sex slaves, his so-called concubines. That was an act of rebellion designed to hurt his father because it meant that David could never again sleep with them (2 Sam 16:20–23).

The norm was that households should be stable, under the firm control of the man of the house and maintained in stability in the interests of the extended family. Sexual intrusions or adventures beyond the marriage and the household of wives and slaves were a major threat. Joseph is, in that sense, the hero because he refused the seductive wiles of Potiphar's wife (Genesis 39). The non-Israelite world was seen as dangerous. It is in this context that we find the prohibitions in Leviticus.

## The Leviticus Prohibitions

With its detailing of laws and regulations that should govern the lives of the people—from procedures of worship to what people should eat—Leviticus addresses what it portrays as abuses within the wider world in which they lived, particularly in relation to sexuality. Incorporated in Leviticus is a block of material, called the Holiness Code (Leviticus 17–27). Within it we find specific regulations relating to sexuality, introduced in Leviticus 18 in the following words:

> The LORD spoke to Moses, saying: Speak to the people
> of Israel and say to them: I am the LORD your God. You
> shall not do as they do in the land of Egypt, where you
> lived, and you shall not do as they do in the land of Ca-
> naan, to which I am bringing you. You shall not follow
> their statutes. (Lev 18:1–3)

It begins in 18:6–16 with prohibitions of incest and, as usual,
addresses men, who are usually the perpetrators. Noah's daughters
are the exception. They made their father drunk in order to sleep
with him and so give them offspring, something they were afraid
they would otherwise never have (Gen 19:32–33).

Sex (and so marriage) was forbidden with one's parents,
their spouses (your stepparents), sisters, stepsisters, sisters-in-law,
daughters, granddaughters, and son's wives. This was fairly comprehensive because, as already noted, a man can otherwise sleep
with anyone else in his household. Marrying a niece is considered
acceptable and became a preferred option for many, although later
this was one of the differences between Pharisees and Essenes.
The latter argued that it should be seen as the same as marrying
one's aunt and so also be forbidden. The rules go on to prohibit
marrying a woman and her daughter (or her son's daughter or her
daughter's daughter and marrying two sisters while both are alive)
(Lev 18:17–18).

Briefly expressed prohibitions follow. "You shall not approach
a woman to uncover her nakedness while she is in her menstrual
uncleanness" (Lev 18:19). Sexual intercourse during menstruation
was forbidden. The grounds for this are the contact with blood,
which should be avoided where possible because it renders a person ritually unclean. It is not always avoidable, however, such as
for a woman during menstruation, and is in no way sinful in itself.
It becomes sinful when you engage in contact with blood where
it could be avoided. There were provisions for purification after
menstruation (Lev 15:19–24) or after any irregular flow of blood
(Lev 15:25–30), childbirth (Lev 12:2–8; taken very seriously in
Luke 2:22–24, 27, 39), and intercourse (Lev 15:18) for women, and

seminal emission (Lev 15:16–17) or any other genital discharge for men (Lev 15:2–15).

The next prohibition is about adultery. "You shall not have sexual relations with your kinsman's wife, and defile yourself with her" (Lev 18:20). Here defilement has a moral quality. The prohibitions continue: "You shall not give any of your offspring to sacrifice them to Molech, and so profane the name of your God: I am the LORD" (Lev 18:21), rejecting child sacrifice. Then follows the prohibition of sex with animals, "You shall not have sexual relations with any animal and defile yourself with it, nor shall any woman give herself to an animal to have sexual relations with it: it is perversion" (Lev 18:23). Unusually, this is addressing not just men's but also women's behavior. Before this prohibition comes the statement that often takes center stage in discussions of same-gender sexual relations: "You shall not lie with a male as with a woman; it is an abomination" (Lev 18:22).

It finds a parallel in Leviticus 20, where we also have a list of prohibitions, this time spelling out the death penalty for adultery and incest.

> If a man commits adultery with the wife of his neighbor, both the adulterer and the adulteress shall be put to death. The man who lies with his father's wife has uncovered his father's nakedness; both of them shall be put to death; their blood is upon them. If a man lies with his daughter-in-law, both of them shall be put to death; they have committed perversion; their blood is upon them. (Lev 20:10–12)

There follows the statement: "If a man lies with a male as with a woman, both of them have committed an abomination; they shall be put to death; their blood is upon them" (20:13). It goes on to add another instance of incest and to repeat the prohibition of sex with animals, again applied to both a man and a woman (Lev 20:14–15).

Much ink has been spilt explaining or seeking to explain what is being referred to in prohibiting a man to "lie with a male as with a woman." The Hebrew can be read as prohibiting a man "to lie the lying of a woman with a man" (i.e., to be the passive partner) or "to lie in the bed of a woman with a man." If the latter, then the prohibition is about a man subjecting himself to be penetrated in anal intercourse by a married man. Given that most men were married, the difference is not great between prohibiting such sex with a married man or prohibiting it with any man. Others have suggested that the two words used, man and male, may suggest that the latter refers only to a heteroerotic male as distinct from a homoerotic one. Such distinctions were not unknown in Akkadian texts, but are not found in Israel's ancient texts. More likely the term "male" is used as a contrast to "female," emphasizing gender difference. This is also how, subsequently, early Jewish writings that applied these prohibitions always read it, as applying to *any* man, and that is likely to be its meaning in the first place.

There is still an ambiguity. Is it referring to a man playing the role of a woman with a man (i.e., being the passive partner) or to a man playing the active role? Either way, there is shame involved. It is shameful for a man to reduce himself to play the role of a woman, deemed inferior, and it is shameful to reduce another man to do so. As the extrapolation in 20:13 indicates, both partners, passive and active, are to be condemned: "both of them have committed an abomination."

Some have noted that in both Leviticus 18 and Leviticus 20 there is reference to the religion of Molech and suggest that it perhaps refers only to such intercourse in a cultic context. Others have suggested that the issue is not moral but ritual uncleanness. Again, this is not how subsequent interpreters read it. On the other hand, in both chapters it comes in the context of prohibiting sex with animals, described in Lev 18:23 as a "perversion." Leviticus 18:22 had described male anal intercourse as an "abomination." Both "perversion" and "abomination" are strong words. An "abomination" is rock bottom among the worst descriptors one could give. It is a word used also of idolatry.

Why "abomination"? The text does not explain. Because it wastes semen and fails the goal of producing offspring? But some things are called an abomination which do produce offspring, such as incest and adultery. Because it makes a man less than a man, a woman, bringing shame on him? Yes, but, more likely, the sense of shame belongs to more than just the contravening of a cultural norm. For it was also to act contrary to what God made a man to be and how he was to engage sexually. That was to be not with another man but with a woman. Whether that perspective was inherent in the prohibition from the beginning is unclear, but it is certainly would have been read that way in the wider context, which included the creation stories.

In that sense the abomination is because the man would be engaging in a perversion of his nature. Men are male and women are female. For a man to be with a man is as bad as a human being with an animal. It runs contrary to nature. That surely made sense in a world where it was obvious where genitals properly belong and fit and what they are for. All men are considered to be heterosexually oriented by nature and for them to behave otherwise is perversion. The biblical authors did not imagine the possibility that some men might be naturally oriented to people of the same sex. They assumed, rather, that all men were heterosexual. So it all made sense. A man being with a man was unnatural and not how God made it to be.

The implications are clear:

> Do not defile yourselves in any of these ways, for by all these practices the nations I am casting out before you have defiled themselves. (Lev 18:21)

> For whoever commits any of these abominations shall be cut off from their people. (Lev 18:29)

We shall explore the way subsequent writers expounded and expanded upon these prohibitions in seeking to differentiate themselves from the non-Jewish world and expose its evils. Before we do so, we turn first to other passages in the Hebrew Scriptures which have sometimes been taken to refer to same-gender sexual relationships.

## More to Come?

### *David and Jonathan?*

As there have been attempts to explain away the prohibitions in Leviticus, so there have been attempts to find positive allusions to same-gender sexual relations elsewhere within the Old Testament. A favorite instance is the love between David and Jonathan. "The soul of Jonathan was bound to the soul of David, and Jonathan loved him as his own soul" (1 Sam 18:1) and "Jonathan made a covenant with David, because he loved him as his own soul" (1 Sam 18:3). "Saul's son Jonathan took great delight in David" (1 Sam 19:1). Saul is reported as confronting his son, Jonathan with the words: "'You son of a perverse, rebellious woman! Do I not know that you have chosen the son of Jesse to your own shame, and to the shame of your mother's nakedness?'" (1 Sam 20:30). On Jonathan's death, David is reported as composing a lament. It included the words: "I am distressed for you, my brother Jonathan; greatly beloved were you to me; your love to me was wonderful, passing the love of women" (2 Sam 1:26).

Does this mean they were also in a same-gender sexual relationship, attracted to each other homo-erotically? Were more than just close friends? Saul's accusation, cited above, suggests shame related to choosing David as a mate. Was it because he saw the relationship between Jonathan and David as sexual? The likelihood is that the authors would not have seen this as a gay relationship, especially given the prohibitions. This coheres with how the story is referred to by later Jewish authors up to the end of the first century CE, such as Josephus. There are no signs of them reading it as a gay relationship, nor of their seeking to counter such a reading as though it had come to mind or been proposed. Close friendships occur between men and between women and it is a preoccupation, especially in recent times, to want to sexualize them wherever they occur. The limited evidence of the text does not allow us to go beyond closeness and intimacy, whatever we might want to imagine into the silence as possibilities.

# The Old Testament

## Sodom and Gomorrah

In discourse about homosexuality the word "sodomy" refers to anal intercourse. It derives from the name of the town, Sodom, paired with Gomorrah. Already in Genesis 13 we read that "the people of Sodom were wicked, great sinners against the LORD" (13:13) and in Genesis 18:20, the text has God declare: "How great is the outcry against Sodom and Gomorrah and how very grave their sin! I must go down and see whether they have done altogether according to the outcry that has come to me; and if not, I will know" (Gen 18:20–21).

To this point there is no explanation about the nature of their sin. The two angels who, according to the story, were visiting Abraham and conveyed this message, then visited Lot in Sodom, who pressed them to stay overnight with him. The story continues: "But before they lay down, the men of the city, the men of Sodom, both young and old, all the people to the last man, surrounded the house; and they called to Lot, 'Where are the men who came to you tonight? Bring them out to us, so that we may know them'" (Gen 19:4–5). In this context "know" has a sexual meaning: "have sexual intercourse with," in this instance, rape them. Instead, for us appallingly, Lot offers them his daughters: "Lot went out of the door to the men, shut the door after him, and said, 'I beg you, my brothers, do not act so wickedly. Look, I have two daughters who have not known a man; let me bring them out to you, and do to them as you please; only do nothing to these men, for they have come under the shelter of my roof'" (Gen 19:6–8). The men wanted to rape the strangers but, being angels, they rescued Lot. They blinded the assailants and sent him, his wife, his daughters, and his prospective sons-in-law on their way the next morning to avoid being killed when God destroyed the city.

Their sin, an act of inhospitality, was to intend sexual violence: male rape. Subsequently, people read into the text more than this. They identified the wickedness of Sodom as engagement in anal intercourse, not just as an act of aggression and domination but also as a consensual act. Hence, the creation of the word "sodomy" to refer to all anal intercourse between men, consensual or not.

There is a parallel story relating to a Levite and his host who were threatened because "the men of the city, a depraved lot, surrounded the house, and started pounding on the door. They said to the old man, the master of the house, 'Bring out the man who came into your house, so that we may have intercourse with him'" (Judg 19:22). It is a terrible story. For the man responded:

> "Here are my virgin daughter and his concubine; let me bring them out now. Ravish them and do whatever you want to them; but against this man do not do such a vile thing." But the men would not listen to him. So the man seized his concubine, and put her out to them. They wantonly raped her, and abused her all through the night until the morning. (Judg 19:24–25)

She survived and made it back to the door of the house where her master found her dead, took her home, then cut her into twelve pieces and had messengers carry her body parts out to all Israel, with the instruction: "Thus shall you say to all the Israelites, 'Has such a thing ever happened since the day that the Israelites came up from the land of Egypt until this day? Consider it, take counsel, and speak out'" (Judg 19:30).

Rape of women and men in war was (and alas, still is) not uncommon. It was also not uncommon within society and could also be a way of acquiring a wife. The story of Jacob's daughter, Dinah, who set out to visit women in the region, illustrates what could occur. "When Shechem son of Hamor the Hivite, prince of the region, saw her, he seized her and lay with her by force. And his soul was drawn to Dinah, daughter of Jacob; he loved the girl, and spoke tenderly to her. So Shechem spoke to his father Hamor, saying, 'Get me this girl to be my wife'" (Gen 34:2–4).

Fathers arranged marriages, so Hamor approached Jacob. Jacob's sons, also important males, joined the negotiation, which was to lead to marriage between the two groups (Gen 34:8–9). The story includes the trap set by the brothers to persuade Hamor's male subjects to be circumcised, but then slaughtered them when they were recovering from the operation, much to their father's disapproval. The story nevertheless reflects a norm after rape. The man was obliged to marry the woman he raped. Never mind about her feelings!

> If a man meets a virgin who is not engaged, and seizes her and lies with her, and they are caught in the act, the man who lay with her shall give fifty shekels of silver to the young woman's father, and she shall become his wife. Because he violated her he shall not be permitted to divorce her as long as he lives. (Deut 22:28–29)

There were also rules which permitted a woman captured in war to be made one's wife.

> When you go out to war against your enemies, and the LORD your God hands them over to you and you take them captive, suppose you see among the captives a beautiful woman whom you desire and want to marry, and so you bring her home to your house: she shall shave her head, pare her nails, discard her captive's garb, and shall remain in your house for a full month, mourning for her father and mother; after that you may go in to her and be her husband, and she shall be your wife. (Deut 21:10–13)

Women were vulnerable in war. This was effectively rape. There were, however, some limits: "But if you are not satisfied with her, you shall let her go free and not sell her for money. You must not treat her as a slave, since you have dishonored her" (Deut 21:14).

## Noah, Drunk and Vulnerable?

Another instance where homosexuality may be in view is when Noah was drunk, lay naked on his bed, and his son Ham looked at him naked and told his brothers (Gen 9:20–27). The text reports: "When Noah awoke from his wine and knew what his youngest son had done to him, he said, 'Cursed be Canaan; lowest of slaves shall he be to his brothers'" (Gen 9:24–25). What had he done that caused Noah to curse Ham's offspring? Just that he looked voyeuristically? Or does it mean he raped his father anally? The text does not resolve the uncertainty. The passages is designed to validate the disparagement of Canaanites, Canaan's descendants, so may be deliberately appalling.

## Male Prostitution?

There may be evidence of male prostitution in some texts. Deuteronomy forbids prostitution:

> None of the daughters of Israel shall be a temple prostitute; none of the sons of Israel shall be a temple prostitute. You shall not bring the fee of a prostitute or the wages of a male prostitute into the house of the LORD your God in payment for any vow, for both of these are abhorrent to the LORD your God. (Deut 23:17–18)

The word translated "male prostitute" in 23:18 is also the word for "dog" and perhaps implies male prostitutes engaging in anal sex. We find reference to such male temple prostitutes elsewhere (1 Kgs 14:24; 15:12; 22:46; 2 Kgs 23:7; Job 36:13–14). It appears that cults existed where such practices formed part of their offerings, perhaps to raise funds, as the prohibition in Deuteronomy implies. The word in Hebrew for a female temple prostitute was *qedeshah*, the same stem as the word for "holy," *qadosh*.

Authors used the image of going after prostitutes to confront Israel for its going after other gods (e.g., Jer 5:7; Hos 4:14; 9:1; Exod 34:15–16; Lev 17:7; 20:5; Deut 7:1–6) instead of remaining faithful to Yahweh as in a marriage.

## Same-Gender Sexual Relations in the Old Testament?

Viewed as a whole, the possible references in the Old Testament to same-gender sexual relations are very few, the clearest being the prohibitions in Leviticus. The assumption in ancient Israel seems to have been that all human beings are heterosexual, so that God-given natural sexual desire was for the opposite sex and that same-gender sexual desire and activity was unnatural and contrary to how God created humans to be.

# 3

# Jewish Writings Outside
# the Hebrew Bible

IN THIS CHAPTER WE explore attitudes towards sexuality in Jewish writings that have survived from the late fourth century BCE to the end of the first century CE. Again, our focus will be on listening to them in their contexts and attending especially to what, if anything, they were saying about same-gender sexual relations. That subject is addressed mainly by writings composed in settings where Jews were a minority confronted by a wider secular culture with which they needed to come to terms and which they could see both as a source of wisdom and as a source of danger and depravity.

I have grouped the potentially relevant documents under four headings. First, under "Writings from Home," are writings most likely to have been composed in the lands of the Jews, some of them sectarian, others, the work of learned priests. All of them reflect how they understood and interpreted their ancient faith. Under the second group, "The Apocrypha," I include two writings that are part of the Apocrypha, Ben Sira and the Wisdom of Solomon. In the third group, "Writings from Abroad," I include writings such as Pseudo-Phocylides and the Sibylline Oracles, which, like already the Wisdom of Solomon, were composed outside of traditional Jewish territory, namely out in the wider world of the Roman Empire. In the final group, Philo and Josephus, we consider the extensive writings of Philo of Alexandria and Josephus, who wrote in Rome. Directly or indirectly, all give us an insight into how Jews in these settings saw matters related to sexuality, and that includes how they interpreted the relevant biblical material.

There is inherent value in listening to these texts, but also because they give us an indication of likely attitudes of Jews in Jesus' day and the period when the New Testament authors wrote, especially Paul, who is a major source for our discussion.

## Writings from Home

The period from the late fourth century BCE to the end of the first century CE was one of creative writing and strong appeals to ancient tradition. Claims to new revelation and insight usually come to us in the form of writings written in the name of a hero of the past. The latest writing to be included still in the collection we call the Hebrew Scriptures or the Old Testament is the Book of Daniel, written during the revolt led by Judas Maccabeus against the Hellenistic Syrian King Antiochus IV Epiphanes, 167–64 BCE. Daniel is a figure of the sixth century BCE. The Book of Daniel belongs in the category of writings attributed to great figures of the past and written in their name, not as forgeries, but seeking to convey what the writers believed would have been the words of these great figures or imagined what they would have said or seen. In this way the collection of wisdom sayings in Proverbs was attributed to Solomon and the first five books of the Bible were attributed to Moses—even though they report his death, but everyone knew how this system of honoring the past and claiming its authority worked.

When we turn to literature outside the Hebrew Scriptures, we have some works that come from much earlier than the Daniel. One celebrated collection, 1 Enoch, is attributed to the patriarch Enoch, of whom Genesis says: "Enoch walked with God; then he was no more, because God took him" (Gen 5:24). That suggested to some that he did not die but instead went straight into the heavenly realms and from there could provide secret information. Imagine what he saw and heard? They did!

### 1 Enoch

We begin our exploration with 1 Enoch. It is a collection of writings attributed to Enoch, some of which go back probably to the late fourth century BCE. These writings appear to have been composed in certain priestly circles in order to inform and inspire followers in their faith. The collection as a whole, called 1 Enoch, survives in full only in the Ge'ez language of Ethiopia, where it is considered to be part of the canon of the Old Testament. We have copies of parts of 1 Enoch also in Greek and in its original language, Aramaic. Copies of the latter were found in the library discovered in the caves by the Dead Sea at Qumran.

Sexual themes appear in some of these writings. In one of the earliest, the Book of the Watchers, 1 Enoch 1–36, we have an elaborate version of a myth found already in Genesis 6. There it serves to explain the origin of legendary giants, called Nephilim. They came about because some angels, understood as male (the usual understanding of angels' gender), came down and slept with women. While Genesis 6 simply reports this without comment, the implication is that this was very wrong and belonged to the start of a downhill slide. That led to God's act of judgement, drowning all but Noah and his family and a select number of creatures in a great flood.

What is implied in Genesis 6 becomes very explicit in the Book of the Watchers. The action of the angels was not only inappropriate; it was serious sin. It not only led to the birth of giants, but created great chaos as they fought each other and, in the process, caused havoc and exploitation among earth's inhabitants. Worse was then to come, because out of their corpses came unclean or evil spirits who from then on roamed the earth bringing physical and mental illness described as demon possession, and who led leaders of foreign nations to become Israel's enemies. This myth helped people explain their ills. Accordingly, it informed what healing meant. It meant driving out demons. This was how people came to see human need and what they understood was happening in acts of healing. Many of Jesus' healings come to us with such explanations. By the Spirit Jesus was casting out demons and setting people free (Matt 12:28; Luke 11:20).

In its descriptions of the evils that this sinful action of the angels brought about, there is surprising little said about sexual sins. At most there is an implicit warning that Israelites should not intermarry with foreigners because they, especially their women, practice witchcraft and sorcery, taught them by the angels. On the other hand, the root cause of all this evil was directly sexual. Angels should never have had sex with human women, acting contrary to their created nature, just as humans should never have sex with animals. Such a mixing of species was an abomination. If you go wrong in the way you handle your sexuality, disaster is bound to follow.

Did they apply this to what Leviticus described as an abomination, men having sex with men and so acting contrary to their created nature? Largely they did not. Only much later in a writing called The Testament of the Twelve Patriarchs, written originally around the turn of the millennia as advice given by each of Jacob's twelve sons to their descendants, do we find that connection made.

In the Book of the Watchers, we read how God told Enoch to reprimand these angels. Accordingly, he reminds them that they are eternal by nature as angels. They do not die. Therefore, they do not need to engage in sexual intercourse and reproduce. They do not need women. It is a rather narrow understanding of sexual intercourse as justified only for purposes of reproduction, but it stays with the basic assumption: act according to your created nature. To do otherwise is both pointless and to disobey God.

Enoch also scolds the angels because, as priests, they should not have abandoned their sacred duties, let alone rendered themselves ritually unclean through sexual intercourse. Priests of the earthly temple were usually married, appropriately engaged in sexual intercourse with their wives, and then observed the usual provisions of being rendered ritually clean through ablutions. That was never sinful. It was sinful to render oneself unclean when it was inappropriate to do so. That, too, was part of the angels' sin. Behind this is an understanding that the heavenly world contains sacred space, a temple.

Nakedness and elements deemed ritually unclean, such as seminal emission, have no place in temples or sacred spaces. Later this would lead to the view that we see reflected in the Book of Revelation and generally among the first followers of Jesus that the world to come would in its entirety be a sacred place, a temple, carrying with it the implication that sex would have no place. Hence Mark's reporting a saying of Jesus which declared: "For when they rise from the dead, they neither marry nor are given in marriage, but are like angels in heaven" (Mark 12:25).

This had the potential to cause confusion, so that we find Paul having to challenge a view that some at Corinth promoted, namely that if we are to be celibate in the age to come, then we should all be celibate now. The fact that he chose celibacy for himself helped fuel this notion, so that he must insist in 1 Corinthians 7 that, on the contrary, marriage and sexual relations in marriage belonged to God's good creation, even if, as he believed, this creation would soon come to an end. We shall return to that discussion in chapter 6 below.

Sexual wrongdoing was, it seems, a continuing concern among Jewish writers in the latter centuries BCE and the first century CE. What they would have seen as the sin of same-gender sex, however, hardly features among these concerns.

## The Book of Jubilees

The Book of Jubilees, written in the first half of the second century BCE, retells the main stories of Genesis and the beginning of Exodus. It is an important source of information about how some circles of faith saw these stories and what they meant for their own day, including in relation to sexuality. It shares much in common with the early writings in 1 Enoch but gives more attention to connecting the latter's insights to the stories of Genesis and early Exodus and also to the laws that follow.

It, too, retells the myth of the angels having sex with women but before that it provides a retelling of the creation of man and woman. In doing so it portrays the man as looking at the animals coming together in pairs in companionship and mating and depicts him as also wanting a companion. God, then, agrees and so woman is created as his partner. God brings her to the man, in contrast to Genesis, which has God bring the man to the woman. Overall, this is a very positive approach to sexual relations.

In Jubilees, the Garden of Eden is a sacred place, a sanctuary. This means that Adam and Eve cannot engage in sexual relations while they are in the garden but had already done so before they entered and did so again only after they departed. This connects to the view that future paradise, the world to come, would be a temple, and thus rendering sexual intercourse out of place there, as we have noted above.

Jubilees gives major emphasis to marriage and companionship as it retells the stories of the patriarchs. It is careful to remove any hint of incest, such as by making it clear that Sarah was Abraham's niece. It constantly insists that Jews should marry only Jews, never foreigners, even those willing to convert. It takes the story of Dinah's abduction in Genesis 34 as a platform for expounding the evils of mixed marriages. As to be expected, another account of her abduction, found in the Aramaic Levi Document, also from the same era, lays some of the blame on Dinah herself—blame the woman!

Jubilees' retelling of the myth of the lusting angels emphasizes that their sin was to act contrary to their created nature, the kind of sin which unleashes disaster. It makes, however, no connection with the prohibition of same-gender relations. That topic is completely absent from the work, as is any discussion of divorce, bestiality, or sex during menstruation.

## The Dead Sea Scrolls

The Dead Sea Scrolls is the name given to documents that began to be discovered in caves near the Dead Sea from 1947 onwards. Many of the documents found there were already well known, for instance, the books of the Old Testament. Others, like some of the writings in the 1 Enoch collection and Jubilees, were also previously known. Some of the scrolls not previously known appear to have belonged to a movement within Judaism identified by the historian Josephus, writing in the late first century BCE, as the Essenes. Like the Pharisees, but even stricter, they lived in cities, but usually kept themselves separate, living in their own enclaves. The ruins found near the caves appear to have been a site where these Essenes sometimes gathered for festivals and special occasions, though some resided there permanently. It appears that they hid their collection of scrolls in the caves when the Romans swept down to their region as they suppressed the revolt that had begun in 66 CE and before they finally retook Jerusalem in 70 CE.

Some of sectarian documents found among them show influence from Jubilees and many share its concern with intermarriage. Many reflect conflicts that the group had with others, especially with the temple priesthood, from which, it appears, some had broken away to form the movement. The conflicts included allegations against their opponents relating to sexual wrongdoing, in particular, that as priests and temple authorities they were lax and in error in interpreting the law. Often the accusations are very general, but we can identify some matters being addressed, such as incest and polygyny. They read the prohibition of a man marrying his aunt as also implying that he must not marry his niece, a position vigorously resisted by the Pharisees and others, who favored having men marry their nieces. The latter saw it as a good way of keeping marriages within the extended family and household.

The Temple Scroll, a document that may predate the foundation of the movement, includes in its regulations for a king, that he have only one wife. The Damascus Document, one of their documents, found also independently in a storeroom of a Cairo synagogue, extends this rule to apply to all Jews. It therefore rejected what had hitherto been a norm, namely having more than one wife. Part of the justification for this ruling was that Leviticus declares that one may not marry two sisters, which it took to mean two Israelite women. Another argument was that the animals went into Noah's ark two by two. It also read Gen 2:24 about a man leaving his household and being joined to his wife as implying that he could have only one wife.

Sometimes the documents express dissent with respect, as in the writing called 4QMMT, which details arguments against mixed marriages. (The letters MMT are the first letters of its Hebrew title. Q stands for Qumran, 4 means cave 4, and b is one of the manuscripts.) In 4QMMTb 75–82 we find an argument based on Lev 19:19. It prohibits letting different types of animals interbreed, sowing different kinds of seeds in one's field, and wearing garments made of different materials (similarly, Deut 22:9–11). Following this principle, different kinds of people, Jews and non-Jews, were also not to mix.

In later writings, I suspect due to their being written during times of heightened alienation, the attacks are general and far less polite. They focus not on countering arguments but on denigrating opponents. They give us, then, little information about why the authors held particular views on sexual wrongdoing. Many of the laws in dispute relate to matters of ritual purity and reflect a strongly priestly mindset and its concerns. Failure to observe ritual purity properly became, accordingly, a matter of morality.

References to same-gender sexual relations are rare in these documents. One document cites the Leviticus prohibition in a list of sins but with no further elaboration (4QDe/4Q270 2 ii.16b–17a / 6QD/6Q15 5 3–4). Similarly, the prohibition of cross-dressing (Deut 22:5) receives mention and is interpreted to apply both to inner and outer garments (4QOrda/4Q159). Sodom and Gomorrah's sin is described as involving "disgusting acts, spending the night together and wallowing" (4QCatenaa/4Q177 9–10; 4QBéat/4Q525 22). This is probably alluding to same-gender sexual acts, but no detail is given. Otherwise, there are no specific references to the nature of the cities' sins.

## The Apocrypha

### Ben Sira/Sirach

Ben Sira, the work of a sage writing around 180 BCE, is now found in the Old Testament Apocrypha. It stands in succession to the Book of Proverbs in addressing issues of sexual wrongdoing. It develops the image in Proverbs of God's Wisdom as a woman, the counterpart of the prostitute soliciting clients on the street. Thus, according to Proverbs, Wisdom calls men to be her lovers (Proverbs 9). In Ben Sira it is similar, but the imagery is at times strikingly erotic. Ben Sira's grandson in translating the work into Greek, the version in which it is now best preserved, mostly rendered such erotic reference more "respectable." He did the same to his grandfather's work as the Greek translators of Proverbs had done, toning down much of the sexually explicit material. Both works, Proverbs and Ben Sira, strongly warn against adultery and sexual wrongdoing. Ben Sira highlights prostitution in particular. Neither addresses matters pertaining to homosexuality.

The focus on same-gender sexual relations comes more to the fore in works that were composed by Jews living within strongly Hellenistic settings, such as in Alexandria in Egypt. There, same-gender sexual relations featured among what such writers saw as signs of the depravity of foreign culture, alongside idolatry and infanticide.

### The Wisdom of Solomon

Standing in the same tradition as Ben Sira is the writing entitled The Wisdom of Solomon, probably written in Alexandria and also in the Apocrypha. It appeals to its readers to be heard as the wise words of King Solomon but, in reality, was composed in the first century BCE by someone well-educated enough to write in fine

Greek style and who reflected the influence of popular Hellenistic philosophy. It alludes to the inhospitality of the people of Sodom, but, like Ben Sira (16:8), does so without making reference to its sexual sins (Wis 10:6–8; 19:13–17). It does, however, make much of the sinfulness of pagan society of its own day, making a connection between its perverse idolatry and its perverse behavior: "For the idea of making idols was the beginning of fornication [sexual wrongdoing], and the invention of them was the corruption of life" (Wis 14:12), which it goes on to expound, concluding:

> For whether they kill children in their initiations, or celebrate secret mysteries, or hold frenzied revels with strange customs, they no longer keep either their lives or their marriages pure, but they either treacherously kill one another, or grieve one another by adultery, and all is a raging riot of blood and murder, theft and deceit, corruption, faithlessness, tumult, perjury, confusion over what is good, forgetfulness of favors, defiling of souls, sexual perversion, disorder in marriages, adultery, and debauchery. (Wis 14:23–26)

In its summary it states: "For the worship of idols not to be named is the beginning and cause and end of every evil" (Wis 14:27). It is likely that the word "sexual perversion" (Wis 14:26) in the list above refers to same-gender sexual acts, listed among a range of other perversions, which were seen as part of the impact of engaging in idol worship and failing to acknowledge the one true God. One perversion, a perverted understanding of God, leads to another: perverted people and behavior.

## Writings from Abroad

### Pseudo-Phocylides

Another piece of fine Greek writing, indeed 231 lines of Greek poetry written in ancient Ionic dialect, and purporting to be the work of a sixth- or seventh-century BCE Greek moral philosopher, Phocylides of Miletus, is Pseudo-Phocylides. It is widely held to have been composed sometime between the late first century BCE and the early first century CE. Quite early on, it addresses sexual wrongdoing as part of its exposition of the prohibitions of the Ten Commandments. It cites them in the sequence in which they occur in the Greek translation of Deuteronomy: adultery, murder, and theft. It became common to use each commandment as a heading under which to include related matters. Thus, it reads: "Neither commit adultery nor rouse homosexual passion" (Ps.-Phoc. 3). Literally it reads: "nor rouse Cypris [=Aphrodite]," alluding to her role in arousing homoerotic passion in Greek mythology.

The author later returns to the theme:

> Go not beyond natural sexual unions for illicit passion
> [literally: Cypris=Aphrodite];
> unions between males are not pleasing even to beasts.
> And let women not mimic the sexual role of men at all.
> (Ps.-Phoc. 190–92)

Here we see the extension of what we find in Leviticus about males engaging in anal sex to illicit passion and its expression, unspecified, between males. It also extends the prohibition to apply to women, thus bringing lesbian sexual relations, the passions and the actions, under condemnation. Interestingly, the author cites a ground for opposing same-gender sex put forward also by Plato, namely that no such thing occurs in the animal kingdom (*Laws* 836C), something we now know to be erroneous.

The author also warns against the dangers of pedophiles:

> Do not grow locks in the hair of a male child.
> Braid not his crown or the cross-knots on the top of his head.
> For men to wear long hair is not seemly, just for sensual women.
> Protect the youthful beauty of a handsome boy;
> for many rage with lust for sex with a male. (Ps.-Phoc. 210–14)

These are just some of the plethora of instructions in relation to sexuality. Others include encouragement to marry: "remain not unmarried, lest you perish nameless, and give something to nature yourself: beget in turn as you were begotten" (175–76); and many warnings against having your wife act as a prostitute (177);

adultery (177–78); incest (179–83); abortion and exposure of infants (184–85); striking one's wife when she is pregnant (186); castration of males (187); sex with animals (188); outraging "a woman by shameful acts of sex" (189); lack of control of one's passions ("Be not inclined to utterly unrestrained lust for a woman. For *Erōs* is no god, but a passion destructive of all" 193–94); rape ("Let no one have sex with maidens forcibly (or) without honourable wooing" 198); marrying evil, wealthy women (199–204); and having multiple marriages ("Do not add marriage to marriage, calamity to calamity" 205).

Positively, the author affirms loving one's wife: "Love your wife: for what is sweeter and better than when a wife is lovingly disposed to her husband into old age and husband to his wife, and strife does not split them asunder?" (195–97); being gentle in bringing up children (207–9); and guarding virgin daughters: "Guard a virgin in closely shut chambers, and let her not be seen before the house until her wedding day. The beauty of children is hard for parents to protect" (215–17).

## Sibylline Oracles and Other Jewish Writings

The concern with same-gender sexual relationships finds expression in other Jewish writings of the time. Often it takes the form of attacking pedophilia, male prostitution of boys, alongside male-male sexual relations generally. We see these concerns in the Sibylline Oracles Book 3 (second century BCE). It is another Jewish writing imitating Hellenistic literature, namely purporting to be the poetic oracles of the legendary priestess, Sibyl. Many such volumes, claiming to be prophesies of the Sibyl, appeared over the next nine centuries. These were written by Jews and then, also, Christians. In the earliest volume, now called Book 3, we read: "Male will have intercourse with male and they will set up boys in houses of ill-fame and in those days there will be a great affliction among men" (3.185–87). In contrast it affirms faithful Jews:

> Greatly, surpassing all men, they are mindful of holy
> wedlock, and they do not engage in impious (or: impure,
> immoral) intercourse with male children, as do Phoe-
> nicians, Egyptians, and Romans, spacious Greece and
> many nations of others, Persians and Galatians and all
> Asia, transgressing, the holy law of immortal God, which
> they transgressed. (Sib. Or. 3.594–600)

Like Wisdom, it sees such behavior as the result of engaging in
idolatry. Book 4 (late first century CE) condemns "hateful and
repulsive abuse of a male" and Book 5 (late in the first century CE
or early second) condemns Rome: "With you are found adulteries
and illicit intercourse with boys. Effeminate and unjust, evil city"
(Sib. Or. 5.166–67; similarly, 5:430) and cites a whole range of acts
of sexual wrongdoing:

> Matricides, desist from boldness and evil daring, you
> who formerly impiously catered for pederasty and set
> up in houses prostitutes who were pure before, with
> insults and punishment and toilsome disgrace. For in
> you mother had intercourse with child unlawfully, and
> daughter was joined to her begetter as bride. In you
> also kings defiled their ill-fated mouths. In you also evil
> men practiced bestiality. Be silent, most lamentable evil
> city, which indulges in revelry. For no longer in you will
> virgin maidens tend the divine fire of sacred nourishing
> wood. (Sib. Or. 5.386–96)

Earlier Pseudo-Aristeas (late second century BCE) was written in the name of a highly esteemed envoy of Ptolemy II Phila-
delphus, who was sent to Jerusalem to meet with the high priest. It
alludes to perversions (Ps.-Aristeas 130, 142), spelling this out in
relation to pedophilia:

> The majority of other men defile themselves in their
> relationships, thereby committing a serious offense, and
> lands and whole cities take pride in it: they not only
> procure the males, they also defile mothers and daugh-
> ters. We are quite separated from these practices. (Ps.-
> Aristeas 152)

Pedophilia, especially in the form of male procurement of young slaves for sexual gratification, and male prostitution were apparently widespread in the Greco-Roman world and seen by Jewish writers as evidence of depravity. The writer of 2 Enoch (early first century CE) depicts men facing judgement, "who practice on earth the sin which is against nature, which is child corruption in the anus in the manner of Sodom" (2 En. 10:2). By this time, Sodom was thus seen as a hotbed of pedophilia. We can notice also the argument that such behavior was unnatural, that is, contrary to how God created people to be. In another place 2 Enoch speaks of human "wickednesses and abominable fornications, that is, friend with friend in the anus, and every other kind of wicked uncleanness which it is disgusting to report" (2 En. 34:2). This goes beyond pedophilia to condemn consenting male-male anal penetration. Sometimes the focus of such condemnation is not on anal intercourse but simply mutual passion, as in the Apocalypse of Abraham (late first century CE), which describes what is apparently adult-to-adult male consensual sex as naked men stand forehead to forehead (Apoc. Abr. 24:8).

Reference to Sodom in the context of such sexual wrongdoing occurs also in the Book of Biblical Antiquities, sometimes called Pseudo-Philo (first century CE), which makes a connection between the rape of the Levite's concubine at Nob and the attempt at violent rape in Sodom (Ps.-Philo 45:1–6). Theodotus sees a connection between the latter and the abduction of Dinah by Shechem (Theod. 7). 2 Baruch (late first century CE) makes a connection with Manasseh's sexual violence against women (2 Bar. 64:2).

The Testaments of the Twelve Patriarchs, in its present form edited by Christian hands, derives from the second or third century CE. Most of its material, however, apart from the Christian additions, comes from much earlier, well back into the first century CE at least. The advice it has Jacob's twelve sons give to their descendants ranges widely, but include issues of sexuality. Reuben, who raped his father's concubine, Bilhah, is presented as giving advice about sexual wrongdoing and the danger, it alleges, that women present to men because of their sexuality.

The author of the Testaments follows a well-worn path of depicting sin and perversion as the result of having a perverted understanding of God. The Testament of Naphtali depicts gay sexual acts as the result of denying God's created order and cites, as examples of such perversion, the Watchers who behaved contrary to their created nature and the people of Sodom who did the same (T. Naph. 2:2—3:5). This is similar to the argument in 2 Enoch. The sin of Sodom and Gomorrah was their engagement in male-to-male sexual acts (T. Levi 14:6; T. Naph. 4:1; T. Benj. 9:1).

## Philo and Josephus

### Philo of Alexandria

By far the most prolific Jewish author of the first century CE and the centuries before whose works have survived was Philo of Alexandria (mid first century CE). In volume they exceed the size of the whole New Testament. They are a treasure trove of information about how a Jewish scholar, well acquainted with the Hellenistic philosophy of his day, expounded the value of his Jewish faith. He did so especially through expositions of "the Law" (Hebrew: Torah), the overall name given to the first five books of the Hebrew Scriptures, Genesis to Deuteronomy.

Some of his works deal with key figures like Abraham and Moses, some with regulations and commandments, some with major events like the creation. He frequently treats the stories symbolically, indulging in complex allegories. In all of his writings Philo sought to draw out the wisdom of the Law, which he read in its Greek translation. He also sought to expound it within the context of popular thought of the wider world of his day.

At times, his highly symbolic expositions use names and events as starting points or platforms for his own reflections and concerns. His comments about sexuality belong within this framework, often highlighting what he, like the other Jewish authors we have considered, saw as the depravity of his non-Jewish world. He deplored the abuse of alcohol, the wild parties of those with the means to enjoy them, and it is often in such passages that he includes attacks on sexual abuse.

His depiction of Sodom highlights its sexual promiscuity:

> The land of the Sodomites . . . was brimful of innumerable iniquities, particularly such as arise from gluttony and lewdness, and multiplied and enlarged every other possible pleasure with so formidable a menace that it had at last been consumed by the Judge of All. (*Abraham* 133)

> Not only in their mad lust for women did they violate the marriages of their neighbors, but also men mounted males without respect for the sex nature which the active partner shares with the passive. (*Abraham* 135)

Excess greed, excess liquor, and excess sex go together for Philo. Excess sex means sexual relations contrary to nature, which includes both promiscuity in engaging in illicit relations with women and also men turning to engage with one another sexually. Philo mounts a number of arguments against same-gender sex beside it being contrary to nature. He alleges that it causes impotence and feminizes men, what he calls the "female disease."

> Then, as little by little they accustomed those who were by nature men to submit to play the part of women, they saddled them with the formidable curse of a female disease. For not only did they emasculate their bodies by luxury and voluptuousness but they worked a further degeneration in their souls and, as far as in them lay, were corrupting the whole of mankind. (*Abraham* 136)

For a man to take a woman's passive role meant becoming, in his eyes and the eyes of most in his time, an inferior, like a woman. That was considered demeaning for a male. More than that, such behavior led to cities being depopulated. Men wasted semen. So he writes:

> God, moved by pity for mankind whose Savior and Lover He was, gave increase in the greatest possible degree to the unions which men and women naturally make for begetting children, but abominated and extinguished

this unnatural and forbidden intercourse, and those who lusted for such He cast forth and chastised with punishments not of the usual kind but startling and extraordinary, newly created for this purpose. (*Abraham* 137)

Philo quite often refers to Sodom as an example of such sexual depravity. For him it is clear. All people are heterosexual, so any orientation, passions, and actions that run contrary to that are acts against one's created nature, indeed against God.

In the document, *On the Contemplative Life*, he depicts what he saw as typically going on in debauched parties: "For waiting there are slaves of the utmost comeliness and beauty, giving the idea that they have come not so much to render service as to give pleasure to the eyes of the beholders by appearing on the scene" (*Contempl. Life* 50). He goes on to describe some "who are still boys" and others who are "full-grown lads fresh from the bath and smooth shaven, with their faces smeared with cosmetics and paint under the eyelids and the hair of the head prettily plaited and tightly bound" (*Contempl. Life* 50). "In the background are others, grown lads newly bearded with the down just blooming on their cheeks, recently pets of the pederasts, elaborately dressed up for the heavier services, a proof of the opulence of the hosts as those who employ them know, but in reality of their bad taste" (*Contempl. Life* 52). Unlike in his exposition of Sodom, where the focus is adult male to male consensual gay sex, here the focus is clearly pedophilia, and more: male sex slavery.

The discussion of such parties in this document brings Philo to speak of Plato's portrait of a banquet where philosophical discussion took place, called a "symposium" (literally, a drinking together). Such symposia were the settings for many such discussions and interchanges and, according to the Gospels, also the occasions where Jesus ate with tax collectors and sinners. It was common not only to invite entertainers, but also visiting teachers and philosophers. Philo describes Plato's symposium in the book entitled the *Symposium*, a fictional dialogue, in the following terms: "the talk is almost entirely concerned with love, not merely with love-sickness of men for women, or women for men, passions recognized by the laws of nature, but of men for other males differing from them only in age" (*Contempl. Life* 59).

Philo's main concern is with what he terms "common vulgar love": "the common vulgar love which robs men of the courage which is the virtue most valuable for the life both of peace and war, sets up the disease of effeminacy in their souls and turns into a hybrid of man and woman those who should have been disciplined in all the practices which make for valour" (*Contempl. Life* 60). He expands upon his concern, especially in relation to pedophilia:

> And having wrought havoc with the years of boyhood and reduced the boy to the grade and condition of a girl besieged by a lover it inflicts damage on the lovers also in three most essential respects, their bodies, their souls, and their property. (*Contempl. Life* 61)

> Cities are desolated, the best kind of men who become scarce, sterility and childlessness ensue through the devices of these who imitate men who have no knowledge of husbandry by sowing not in the deep soil of the lowland but in briny fields and stony and stubborn places, which not only give no possibility for anything to grow but even destroy the seed deposited within them. (*Contempl. Life* 62)

Philo was very aware of the view held by some, that being gay was something natural, but rejects that view outright. In his *Symposium*, Plato puts such a view on the lips of one of his characters, Aristophanes (*Symposium* 189–90). It is not Plato's own view, as we shall see later when we turn more directly to his writings, but it made for a stimulating symposium conversation. Aristophanes presents a myth, which recounts that in the beginning there were three kinds of human beings—male, female, and androgynous (male and female at the same time). They offended Zeus who sliced them in half, rearranged their genitals, and ever since the two halves of the male have been longing for each other (male-to-male desire), the two female halves have been doing similarly (female-to-female desire), and the androgynous halves have been doing the same, male and female yearning for each other (hetero-sexual desire).

Philo dismisses it as "seductive enough, calculated by the novelty of the notion to beguile the ear," but to be treated by "the disciples of Moses trained from their earliest years to love the truth . . . with supreme contempt" (*Contempl. Life* 63).

Philo's nephew cites him as saying: "Some resolve to wick-edness and fall into such violent passion for unlawful sexual indulgence that they commit sodomy. They disturb not only com-munities but also the very order of nature. However, truth herself convicts them for transgressing unalterable law, for committing immoral acts, for giving the seed to the immature, and for wasting and destroying the seed" (*Animals* 49).

In his retelling of the story of Noah's ark, Philo emphasizes heterosexual relations as the only legitimate pairing as he describes people's exit from the ark: "But after (the flood) had ceased and come to an end and they had been saved from the evil, He again instructed them through the order (of their leaving the ark) to has-ten to procreate, by specifying not that men (should go out) with men nor women with women but females with males" (*QG* 2.49).

Elsewhere he rails against "the mannish-woman as much as the womanish-man" (*Virtues* 20–21). Like Pseudo-Phocylides, he assumes that the prohibitions of Leviticus apply generally to all same-gender sex, both gay and lesbian.

In his specific exposition of the prohibitions in Leviticus, Philo brings the usual argument, namely that gay sex feminizes men, wastes semen (assumed by him and by many to be in limited supply), and produces absurd spectacles: "Mark how conspicuous-ly they braid and adorn the hair of their heads, and how they scrub and paint their faces with cosmetics and pigments and the like, and smother themselves with fragrant unguents" (*Spec. Laws* 3.37). His target is not just pedophilia but also consensual sex between men. He emphasizes the death penalty required according to Lev 20:13. "These persons are rightly judged worthy of death by those who obey the law, which ordains that the man-woman who debases the sterling coin of nature should perish unavenged, suffered not to live for a day or even an hour, as a disgrace to himself, his house, his native land and the whole human race" (*Spec. Laws* 3.38). He then turns to the active male partner: "And the lover of such may be assured that he is the subject of the same penalty. He pursues an unnatural pleasure and does his best to render cities desolate and uninhabited by destroying the means of procreation" (*Spec. Laws* 3.39).

Philo deplores what he sees as the popularity of such behavior:

> The reason is, I think, to be found in the prizes awarded in many nations to licentiousness and effeminacy. Certainly you may see these hybrids of man and woman continually strutting about through the thick of the market, heading the processions at the feasts, appointed to serve as unholy ministers of holy things, leading the mysteries and initiations and celebrating the rites of Demeter. (*Spec. Laws* 3.40)

> Those of them who by way of heightening still further their youthful beauty have desired to be completely changed into women and gone on to mutilate their genital organs are clad in purple like signal benefactors of their native lands, and march in front escorted by a bodyguard, attracting the attention of those who meet them. (*Spec. Laws* 3.41)

Philo is not an outlier promulgating novel approaches to gay issues. Rather he is enunciating what most of his fellow Jews would have affirmed in rejecting what they saw as the depravity of the non-Jewish world with which they were confronted. Clearly, sex slavery, male prostitution, and male sexual exploitation of minors were major evils. Philo goes also beyond these to attack both men and women who engaged in same-gender sex consensually. It was unnatural, he said. That is, more seriously, it was to think, feel, and act contrary to God's will for oneself in creation. For men, what was even worse—as he, along with so many others, saw it— was that it meant the passive partner had to stoop to the level of a woman. Such behavior by the passive partner and implicating also the active partner was shameful, reducing the superior, the male, to the level of the inferior, the female. The arguments about the dangers of depopulating cities by misdirecting semen and wasting it when it could have been used to produce offspring was also to contravene God's design for creation.

## Josephus

Almost as prolific as Philo was Josephus, the Jewish historian who wrote in the second half of the first century CE. He had been a general in Galilee at the time of the revolt against Rome in 66 CE, was captured, but then managed to ingratiate himself with the Romans. In Rome he wrote accounts of the revolt, *The Jewish War*, and of his people, *The Antiquities of the Jews*, covering history up to his own time. His accounts are an invaluable resource, especially when we have more than one account of the same events, one in each of his main series. He also wrote shorter pieces, including an autobiography. Mostly he describes events, recounting them from his own perspective and bias, which one must at times assess for any distortion it produced. He also wrote expositions and explanations of biblical law, seeking at all times to present his faith in the best light possible to his educated Roman audience.

We see this in the way he reflects his audience's low view of Antony, the rival of Octavian, who became Emperor Augustus, the inaugural leader of the empire. We may know Antony because of his famed romance with Cleopatra, leader of Egypt. Less well known, but relevant for our reflections, is Josephus' account of Antony's philandering and the way it caused grief to Herod the Great in the early years of his reign (37–34 BCE).

When the Romans invaded Judea and associated lands in 64 BCE, they had to deal with a rivalry that had broken out between the two sons of Queen Salome Alexandra (76–67 BCE), widow of Alexander Janneus (103–76 BCE), belonging to the royal house of Hasmon, called the Hasmoneans. The Romans' resolution of the conflict was to side with one of the sons, Hyrcanus. They appointed him high priest and brought in an Idumean warlord, Antipater, to rule with Hyrcanus on their behalf in Jerusalem. Chaos and civil war ensued when the other son, Aristobulus, allied with the invading Parthians, who pressed in from the east in the mid 50s BCE. It was finally Herod, Antipater's son, who quashed the rebellion and so was appointed king by the Romans in 37 BCE.

Alliances between warring partners were often sealed with arranged marriages. Accordingly, the son of Aristobulus, Alexander, married the daughter of Hyrcanus, Alexandra. That was an attempt to restore harmony in the House of Hasmon. Among their children were Mariamme and Aristobulus, named after his paternal grandfather. Herod grasped the opportunity to marry into the Hasmonean dynasty, which was now defunct but still influential, by marrying Mariamme. It became much more than a marriage of convenience. Josephus tells us that Herod fell passionately in love with her, a story worthy of a feature film. It ends with his becoming terribly jealous, executing her, and then bewailing what he had done. It is quaintly pathetic.

Much earlier than that, while Herod made a wise move in marrying Mariamme, he was concerned not to give the surviving House of Hasmon too much power, so instead of appointing Mariamme's brother, Aristobulus, as high priest, which is what one would have expected, he appointed a relatively unknown priest from the Jewish community in Babylonia. Aristobulus' mother, Alexandra, was furious and sent a letter off to Antony and Cleopatra to complain. Antony's envoy came and had portraits painted of both Aristobulus, a very handsome sixteen-year-old, and Mariamme, also very attractive, and took them back to Antony. Josephus suggests that this was to portray them to Antony as worth "having"—in a predatory sexual sense.

Befitting his reputation among the knowing Romans of Josephus's audience, Antony was happy to seize the opportunity, but finally sent only for the boy. Sending for Herod's wife, he realized, would be going a bit far. Herod, alerted to what was happening, immediately dismissed the former high priest and appointed Aristobulus high priest after all. That saved him. Because the rule was that the high priest had to remain in Judea, he couldn't be sent to

Antony in Alexandria. Later, Herod would have him "accidentally" drowned, but at least he saved him from Antony's predatory grasp.

While the story is bizarre, it does reflect the kind of thing that Philo had condemned and Jews found appalling about pagan culture, namely that there were men, often in high and powerful positions, who were sexual predators towards both men and women.

According to Josephus, Herod in his old age used to be attended by eunuchs, a term usually used for castrated males, who were entrusted "with putting the king to bed" (*Ant.* 16.230). He writes that Herod "had some eunuchs of whom he was immoderately fond because of their beauty" (*Ant.* 16.230). Rulers often employed eunuchs as civil servants because they could be sure that, however sexually promiscuous they were—and often they were—they could not make the ruler's wives, female assistants, or sex slaves pregnant. In an act of subversion against his father, one of Herod's sons, Alexander, bribed them to have sexual relations with him. Thus, Alexander was doing to Herod what Absalom had once done to David. Herod was clearly indulging in same-gender sex.

In his exposition of the Law, Josephus affirms sexual intercourse as "the natural union of man and wife [woman], and that, only for the procreation of children" (*Ag. Ap.* 2.199) and so deplores "the practice of sodomy in the pursuit of lawless pleasure" (*Ant.* 3.275) as something brought about by obsession with pleasure and by excess. He condemns men engaging in same-gender sexual acts, especially those taking a passive role, on the ground that "by reason of the effeminacy of their soul that they have changed the sex of their body also. And so with all that would be deemed a monstrosity by the beholders" (*Ant.* 4.290–91). He, too, cites the example of Sodom, explaining that the would-be perpetrators of male rape were taken by the (angels') men's beauty (*Ant.* 1.200). He alleges that those of the Zealot movement, among those who revolted against Rome, were guilty of violation of women and effeminacy, cross-dressing, and copying women's passions (*J.W.* 4.561–62) and makes the same charge against the Emperor Gaius.

Like Philo, Josephus sees such vices as typical of the depraved world but, conforming to Roman prejudice, which often depicted it as a Greek disease, pointed to "unnatural and extremely licentious intercourse with males" in Sparta, Elis, and Thebes (*Ag. Ap.* 2.269, 273–75). He says nothing of female-to-female same-gender sexual relations and his account of David and Jonathan exhibits no trace of his or anyone else's having read it as homoerotic.

## Concluding Reflections

The picture emerging from this array of Jewish literature is relatively coherent. The underlying assumption, surely reasonable in the light of reading Gen 1:27, was that God made humankind male and female and that all human beings are heterosexual. This was their scientific understanding. It was obvious to the onlooker that this is how things were meant to be: male and female genitals are different and designed to fit together. Anything other than that in orientation, passion, and action had to be unnatural and a transgression of the divine order of creation.

Arguments about wasted semen and having one of the male partners reduced to the level of a woman, are secondary concerns, though carried considerable weight in that context.

The condemnation applied to men and to women. It also applied to consensual sexual engagement. Beyond that, there was a keen sense of the evils of pedophilia and sexual slavery and prostitution, despite an assumed tolerance of male householders having sexual rights over all women within their household, aside from what constituted incest. The difference was that in Jewish communities that access applied only to females. In wider society it was sexual access to all, male and female.

Same-gender sexual relations were seen as one of the boundary markers that separated Jews, who rejected them, and the gentile world, which partially accepted them, along with idolatry and such practices as infanticide, abortion, and prostitution. None of the surviving Jewish writings questions these views. They are simply fact, understood by all, and become standard ammunition for those wanting to cite human depravity among those who failed to acknowledge God. We may without doubt assume that the Jews and converts to Judaism who became followers of Jesus, and were involved in the emergence of the Jewish movement that eventually morphed into Christianity, continued to hold these views.

Before we turn to them, we need first to listen to that other world beyond Judaism, because on these matters there were indeed different voices and indications of conflict and controversy.

# 4

# The Greco-Roman World

IN THE PREVIOUS CHAPTER we have already been looking out at the wider world beyond the Jewish community and seeing it through the eyes of writers like Philo and Josephus. There is no need to doubt the information they provide, though it may contain some negative bias.

## Wild Parties

As Philo notes frequently, there were parties among those who could afford them. Fueled by alcohol, all manner of sexual promiscuity could take place. Such parties weren't always orgies, but the fact that some were and were occasions for wrongdoing, including sexual wrongdoing, gave such gatherings a bad name. This also explains the many anecdotes about Jesus facing criticism for eating with tax collectors and sinners (probably women entertainers), and his choosing not to write such people off.

Such parties would sometimes have been simply men reclining together for a drink (the meaning of *symposium*) to engage in conversation, discuss philosophy, hear the latest teacher (like Jesus), or be entertained. Reclining was the fashion and also characterized such gatherings in Jesus' time in Galilee. At the less respectable end, one can imagine such symposia being anything but restrained conferences on philosophy. Flowing wine, female entertainers, including prostitutes (male and female), men reclining close to each other—because they were normally male only, except for the entertainers—were a formula for wild behavior. Thus, in the wider world beyond the Jewish community, as Philo amongst others tells us, that would include all kinds of sexual promiscuity, men with women, and men with men, not least with adolescent boys, often slaves, made to serve their masters' sexual indulgences.

Herod Antipas' birthday party (Mark 6:14–29) allows us to see some typical features of such banquets. The respectable women, like Antipas' new wife, Herodias, are not with the men but in the next room. Her daughter, his stepdaughter, is with them, however, as an entertainer, dancing, and wows Antipas into crass stupidity, as befits such a tale in those times. Probably to be imagined as half drunk, Antipas offers her half his kingdom. She then has to go to the next room to consult her mother. It was not unusual to write about men behaving stupidly in relation to sex, probably because too often it matched reality.

## Prostitution

Philo may be exaggerating when he claims that it was expected of young men from age fourteen onward to visit prostitutes, female or male, for sexual experience (*Joseph* 42), but at least it can be assumed that this practice was widespread. What else should one do with one's sexual proclivities in the years before one was expected to marry around the age of thirty? We may suspect that sexual adventuring would also not have been unknown in Jewish society, though confined to engagement with female prostitutes. We find reference to such prostitutes sprinkled among the stories and sayings of Jesus, so they must have been around.

In the wider world beyond the Jewish community, engagement in same-gender sexual acts was not hushed up, at least in relation to men. People knew it went on. There were brothels of male prostitutes. There were slaves kept for sex, male and female. There were the wild parties and goings on at bath houses, but there were also less public venues, and men acting independently: predatory males and pedophilia. Same-gender sexual scenes were not uncommon on pottery. It was something in the public eye and awareness. Such scenes would be seen from a young age.

## Mentoring and Pedophilia

In some Greek city states it was not uncommon, especially among elites, for older men to mentor adolescent boys. Having a sexual component to one's mentoring of such boys and young men seemed to many to be respectable, for those were close relationships of care and affection. Indeed, such mentoring had its own rules, such as that it should cease when the young man reached marrying age, normally in his late twenties. Then marriage should be arranged for him with a suitable wife.

We noted in the previous chapter that Josephus deplored this form of mentoring in Sparta, Elis, and Thebes (*Ap.* 2.273–75). He wrote of their toleration of "unnatural and extremely licentious intercourse with males," elsewhere speaking of "Greek habits" (*Ap.* 2.269) and pointed to such behavior even among their gods. The Spartans apparently believed that engaging in sex with one another helped build the bonds between soldiers, which they saw as highly desirable for maintaining a sense of solidarity and strength.

In aristocratic circles in Athens, as mentioned above, there was also sometimes a sexual component to the mentoring of adolescent boys. It is not clear that such engagement took the form of anal intercourse with the boy or just rubbing of the penis to ejaculation against his thighs or upper leg, as sometimes depicted on vases. Most handled their sexual contacts with their boys with care so as to avoid having such young men addicted to being anally penetrated and gaining the shameful reputation of being a *kinaidos*—a man preferring to be penetrated. It was shameful because it meant behaving like women and becoming like them, becoming effeminate, a "softy," and losing one's manliness. As in ancient

Israel, women were considered to be inferior to men. How could a man do that to himself! In best practice the mentor should always bear in mind that the young man was also later, usually in his late twenties or early thirties, to get married. In his work the *Phaedrus*, Plato has Socrates warn such mentors about the wild horse of passion and urges that excess be reined in (253D).

## Roman Rules

The Romans, for their part, despised such mentoring practice, labelling it the Greek disease.

Their law, reinforced under Emperor Augustus as the *Lex scatinia*, made having sexual relations with a fellow male citizen or with an unmarried female citizen a criminal offence (*stuprum*). It was also an offence to engage sexually with the women or men belonging to another man's household, let alone with the other man's wife, not least because that entailed theft of another man's property. As in Israel, adultery was strictly outlawed. Emperor Augustus reinforced this with his *Lex Iulia* decree in 18 BCE, requiring prosecution also of any man who failed to bring an adulterous wife to court. Rules were strictly enforced, especially among citizens: no adultery! No sex between men!

It was, however, quite another matter when it came to noncitizens and inferiors. Thus, Roman society officially tolerated prostitution, male and female; sexual abuse of slaves, male and female; same-gender sexual relations, with or without consent, between adults or with minors, as long as it was not between citizens. Unofficially, in liquor fueled wild parties one can imagine that such rules often went by the wayside and sometimes such relations went on among citizens far beyond marriageable age, as we see referred to often in the writings of Philo.

We have already noted Antony's alleged predatory sexual behavior, as reported by Josephus, in wanting to have sex with Herod the Great's attractive wife, Mariamme, and her brother Aristobulus. Accounts of some emperors accuse them of male sexual abuse. Suetonius tells us that Emperor Gaius Caligula was notorious for sexual predation and ended up being stabbed through his genitals, and Nero was little better. There were also rumors of Stoic teachers in Rome who engaged in sexual relations with their students.

While Romans, therefore, deplored what they called the Greek disease, Greeks argued that in fact Romans were to be condemned because they tolerated such relationships beyond when a minor reached marriageable age.

Romans prized strength, courage, and action as the virtues of manliness. They shared with Greek culture a horror of a man being reduced to being passive and female. So, for them, too, it was something terrible for a man to be a *cinaedus* (Greek *kinaidos*), a man wanting to be penetrated. One can imagine that the strong men who engaged in sex with such men also despised them at the same time, and the evidence supports this. *Cinaedi* were seen as a potentially serious threat to society, undermining its strength.

## Plato and the Philosophers

In the previous chapter we had cause to cite Plato because Philo referred to his character in the *Symposium*, Aristophanes, and Aristophanes's theory about the origin of diverse sexual desires. It came from an angry Zeus, who sliced the first man and woman in half. Hence their desire ever since to re-join: men to men, women to women. The rest, the majority, of humanity are descended from a third human who was bisexual, male and female, also sliced in half, hence their desire to re-join by seeking their partners in the opposite sex. Philo gave the myth short shrift and Plato, too, cited it as something he did not believe. The passage is important evidence that some people did believe that there was such a thing as being gay. This is sometimes overlooked by those who see the concept of "homosexuality" coming into use only in recent centuries. There is also other evidence of people recognizing gay orientation, for instance, in astrological texts that indicate that some were born that way.

Plato also wrote adventurously about human reproduction. In his *Republic*, he proposed a new order for society to ensure stable means of high-quality offspring. He suggested abolishing marriage, holding women in common, and then ensuring that those appointed as guardians copulate with them to produce fine offspring, a strategy for selective breeding. An assumption underlying the plan is that women need to be controlled because they generally lack self-control. In the *Timaeus* he suggests that women originated from men who had failed in their former life and so were reduced to a lower level in their next life in the journey of reincarnation. If they kept failing, they might find themselves at some stage in the future reincarnated as mere worms slithering on the ground.

In his work, *Laws*, Plato retreats from his proposed strategy in the *Republic*, and insists instead that people should engage in sexual intercourse only for the sake of reproduction. Semen was not to be wasted: whether by masturbation, by intercourse during menstruation or with contraception, or by engaging with another male. Thus, he opposed same-gender sexual relations, including by arguing that no such thing occurs in the animal kingdom, something we now know to be incorrect. Sex, just for gratification, he argued, should have no place (*Laws* 838E–839A). Philo followed Plato in this view and saw the element of pleasure in intercourse as having its place only because it promoted more effective conception (*Creation* 151–52).

Plato nevertheless conceded that his strict rules should apply only while a woman is fertile and agrees that sexual intercourse may continue afterwards even when no conception was possible, as long as it was not too passionate or excessive (*Laws* 784E3–785A3, 783E4–7, 784B1–3). Philo agreed, acknowledging that it was also an expression of companionship (*Spec. Laws* 3.35). Some were much stricter, like the Neopythagoreans of Philo's time, who insisted that sexual intercourse should only ever be for human reproduction. Some Stoics, like Seneca (mid first century CE) and Musonius Rufus (late first century CE), agreed. The earlier Pythagoreans had drawn attention to the fact that intercourse was the moment when the soul became embodied in matter, so should be handled with care and not done in the turbulence of emotion, which might leave the offspring damaged for life.

By the first century, philosophers like the Stoics became increasingly focused not on the world of ideas but on issues of lifestyle and well-being. It was one of the richest periods in western society for exploring emotions. The most common theme was: *don't do anything to excess*. Excessive pain or joy or desire was destabilizing. Happiness and fulfilment came through balance and control, moderation of one's feelings, whether for sex or food and drink. Such philosophy informed the reflections of Philo and others that one of the reasons why men breach natural boundaries and engage in sex with men is because of excessive passion and failure to control it. Desire, passion, is not wrong; *excessive* passion and *misdirected* passion is. Epicurean philosophers, often misrepresented as blind pleasure seekers, spoke of pleasure in the sense of well-being and how best to achieve it, but did so without appealing to belief in gods or the afterlife.

Early Stoics, such as Zeno of Citium (third century BCE), sought to free sexual relations from the restrictions that they faced. Such restrictions centered on marriage and so forbade adultery, sex between men, sex between women, and incest. These early Stoics, however, believed that such varied sexual encounters were acceptable as long as there was mutual consent. What they did disapprove of was sex with minors, sex purely for self-gratification or monetary gain, and sex outside the context of friendship. The later Stoics retained the emphasis on consent and friendship but drew back to a more traditional view of insisting that sexual intercourse belonged in marriage.

## Men and Households

Certain values were widely held across Greek, Roman, and also Jewish culture (as noted in chapter 1 above) and governed everyday life. The household was paramount. It was the basis of the economy and of human welfare. Nothing should threaten it. The man was the head of the household and had the right of sexual access to all women and men (except in Jewish culture) within the household except where it would constitute incest. There was, as we have seen, no place for adultery, a common view also across Greek, Roman, and Jewish cultures, and adultery required divorce.

Equally, nothing should threaten the head of the household, the man. His manliness must be upheld. He needed to be in control, including not just of his wife, children, and slaves, as the household codes in Colossians and Ephesians remind us (Col 3:18—4:1; Eph 5:21—6:9), but also of himself. He must not be given to excess, in relation to food, drink, sex, and any feeling or emotion that might undermine his stability. He must reproduce. To waste his semen unproductively threatened the household's future, its offspring who will work for it, inherit it, and be there to support any household members who survive into old age.

While some men would have adopted the stances of some of the philosophers and restricted sexual intercourse to relations with their wives and even then, treated it functionally, others had no such qualms. They were a threat, therefore, not just to their household but to society and its future. Weaken the man, the head of the household, and you also weaken society which depends for its stability on strong men, whether as soldiers for war or those responsible for negotiating marriages and alliances for the future and or simply as a key to the survival of the species.

## Manliness, Semen, and Shame

The fear of depopulation because of semen wasted through same-gender sexual relations and potentially running out was widespread. It may strike the modern reader as very odd. It needs, however, to be heard in its setting in the ancient world where mortality rates were high. Life expectancy for women across the Roman Empire in our period is estimated to have been twenty-five to thirty years. More than half the women who lived beyond fifteen years of age would have died before they were forty or perhaps even thirty-five. Many died in childbirth. Without adequate contraception women would have fallen pregnant every two to three years and there was a high rate of child mortality, perhaps every second birth or more. Life expectancy for men was around forty-two to forty-six and, with the high mortality rate of women, often married more than once. Maintaining population growth under these conditions was not easy. Hence the anxiety.

Men needed to take control and be in control, because the underlying assumption that informed society was that men and women were not equal. Purely at the physical level of their genitalia some argued that they were equal, the female having an inverted form of male genitalia, the vagina an inside-out penis. Indeed, some argued that this fit made male-female copulation the only legitimate form of sexual engagement. It was not, however, seen as undermining the basic notion that women were inferior. In reproduction they were, in some theories, mere recipients of the seed sown in their womb. Even when, following Hippocrates, others argued that both produced semen and the gender of the baby was determined by who produced the most, there was no shaking the general assumption of men's superiority. Aristotle saw woman as "a defective male" (*Gen. an.* 737A.28) and, as noted above, Plato speculated that they were incarnating a failed male from a previous life.

The age disparity in most marriages, where the man married around thirty years of age and the woman in her teens, reinforced the sense of superiority. From the observation that their wives were less experienced, men often made a fallacious leap to conclude that they were, by nature, not only not as strong physically, but also weaker intellectually and less able to control their feelings—not least their sexuality—and so needing to be controlled.

Such assumptions, therefore, underlie the shamefulness of a man taking a woman's role by becoming the penetrated one. Rape was, accordingly, a form of subjugation in war, reducing an equal to the level of an inferior, a woman. Men who engaged as passive partners in same-gender sexual intercourse were to be despised—even if they were to be used for gratification.

## Lesbian Relations

Such values made it hard, therefore, to come to terms with female-female sexual relations. They were generally abhorred, despite the popularity among some of the love poetry of Sappho (sixth century BCE) on the island of Lesbos, whose location gave the name to such relationships as lesbian. In such relations the offensive aspect was the opposite to male-male relations. The passive female partner fitted nature's role for women as commonly understood, but the notion of a woman usurping a man's role by acting as the active partner caused males to shudder. We also read of male fantasies of women whose clitoris had grown so grotesquely large as to be able to penetrate another woman's vagina.

Female to female sexual relations met with widespread disapproval by most. Ovid, for instance, who otherwise revels in erotics, declares it unnatural, even in the world of animals (mistakenly), and offensive (Ovid *Met.* 9.728–34).

## Eunuchs

Eunuchs were in a special category in relation to their sexuality. They were generally understood to be males who were impotent and had either been born that way or been castrated. The knowledge that some were born that way may reflect awareness of what, in recent times, we have come to identify as intersex, but they were seen basically as males. Being impotent did not mean they lacked sexual desire, but, not being not able to make women pregnant, they were a safe option for rulers to use as civil servants, courtiers, and sometimes being entrusted with managing harems. They could also perform the functions of the passive partner in same-gender sex—including as male prostitutes—and engage in manual sex acts. The Book of Wisdom declares: "Blessed also is the eunuch whose hands have done no lawless deed" (Wis 3:14). Sometimes the word appears to be used to refer to court officials who need not have been eunuchs in the strict sense.

## Concluding Reflections

There was, therefore, some diversity in attitudes towards same-gender sexual relationships in the wider world beyond Jewish communities. That diversity ranged from wild promiscuity of partygoers exploiting slaves and male prostitutes, to stern rejection of such behavior as depriving the human race of its future by wasting its seed/semen. That diversity existed within a social framework that saw men as superior and households as fundamental, to be preserved almost at all cost. The excesses and the promiscuity appalled Jews, who knew that all people were as God made them, male and female, heterosexual, and should behave accordingly. Jewish moral teaching combined well with the popular philosophies that enjoined control and moderation and living in harmony with nature, which Jews could understand as God's creation, God's law. It should not surprise us to find that the Jewish Jesus movement, which eventually became a Jewish and gentile movement, held fast to such values and the assumptions that underlay them. We turn to this movement in the chapters that follow.

# 5

# The New Testament Outside
# of Paul's Writings

IF WE LOOK AT the New Testament through the eyes of the gentile world, what do we see of same-gender sexual relations?

## A Centurion with a Sex Slave?

Was the centurion's "servant," or more accurately, his slave, whom Jesus healed, according to the story shared by Matthew and Luke (Matt 8:5–13; Luke 7:1–11), his sex slave, as some have suggested? Is that what is implied when the story in Luke notes that the centurion valued him highly? Could that mean he was fond of him, enamored of him? And did the fact that Jesus offered no comment about the relationship imply that he approved?

Such questions raised in relation to the story are probings in the dark, speculation in the silence. Nothing in the story indicates that the slave was a sex slave, although it is possible that a reader familiar with practices in the wider world might have assumed so. Nor does anything indicate that he was not. The likelihood, however, is that he was not. The Greek word used to express that he was valuable (*entimos*) to the centurion will have meant just that, not necessarily that he was enamored of him. To read the story as one about a centurion and his sex slave, let alone as indicating Jesus' approval or indifference, is most probably a misreading. Otherwise, we should expect to find sensitivity to the issue in subsequent retellings of the story in contexts where that would be highly problematic. To my knowledge we find none.

When the centurion declares, "Lord, I am not worthy to have you come under my roof" (Matt 8:8; Luke 7:6), this is not referring to the centurion's guilt about having a sex slave, but about the fact that he was a gentile and that, normally, Law-observant Jews should avoid entering gentile houses. That was the point of the story of Peter's visiting the house of the centurion, Cornelius, in Acts 10. Peter would not have gone except that God instructed him through a vision that it would be acceptable and that gentiles, too, are worthy. The story of the centurion and his slave has its origins in conservative circles, where keeping distance from gentiles was taken seriously. It is noteworthy that Jesus did not go to his house but healed the slave from a distance. This was also what Jesus did, after initial reluctance, in response to the request from the gentile Syro-Phoenician woman who asked for help for her daughter (Mark 7:24–30). He healed her from a distance. Only in anecdotes about gentiles did Jesus heal people from a distance.

In addition, we have what appears to be an independent version of the story in the Gospel according to John. It may or may not be an exception. It tells of a royal official, who may or may not have been a gentile, and his son (John 4:46–54). Jesus healed the man's son from a distance. Like the story of the healing of the centurion's slave, this healing, too, is located in Capernaum. Confusion may have arisen from the fact that one of the words for child is also a word for slave, *pais*, the word Matthew uses in 8:6. This is in contrast to Luke, who uses another word that only means slave. One version may well, then, have spoken of the centurion's son. A centurion, an official? Close enough to be confused. The story in John focuses on the miracle itself and the exact timing of the healing. The story in Matthew and Luke serves to signal openness to gentiles, especially in Matthew. None of the versions give the impression, directly or indirectly, that they are about pedophilia, let alone its approval.

## Jesus and the Children

Another story which might have been heard by gentiles among Mark's hearers, and by subsequent hearers, as reflecting such relationships is the well-loved story of Jesus blessing the children (Mark 10:13–16; retold in Matt 19:13–15). It reports that "people were bringing little children to him in order that he might touch them" (10:13). The word for children here, *paidia*, can mean little children, as some translations render it, but it can also mean older children. A few chapters earlier Mark had used the word of the twelve-year-old daughter of Jairus (5:40). What were parents doing bringing their children to Jesus that he might touch them? Why were the disciples so angry with them? The problem may well be implied in the use of the word "touch." It could have sexual connotations. We see it used in this way by Paul in 1 Corinthians 7:1, when he suggests that given the nearness of the end it is not a good idea for men to touch (i.e., have sex with) women.

Heard in this way, the story might suggest that these parents were doing what sometimes happened with travelling teachers. They were wanting to expose their children to his teaching and influence and that could include having him show their children favors, including fondling them, which might also include sexual touching. Could the story really have been heard in this way? Yes, that was possible. It might make sense of the disciples' stern rebuke.

Is there any evidence that it was read in this way? No, there is not, unless we see it in Matthew's replacement of "touch" by "lay hands on them and pray" (19:13), which removes the suggestive ambiguity of the word "touch." Even less likely is the possibility that the story carried these implications when Mark was retelling it or in its earlier forms. Again, we are dealing with speculation in the dark. A story about potential pederastic behavior? Very unlikely. And it is certainly not what Jesus goes on to do. Mark reports that Jesus rebuked the disciples:

> But when Jesus saw this, he was indignant and said to them, "Let the little children come to me; do not stop them; for it is to such as these that the kingdom of God belongs. Truly I tell you, whoever does not receive the kingdom of God as a little child will never enter it." And he took them up in his arms, laid his hands on them, and blessed them. He responded: "Truly I tell you, whoever does not receive the kingdom of God as a little child will never enter it." And he took them up in his arms, laid his hands on them, and blessed them. (Mark 10:14–16)

Would pedophilia anyway have been far from the minds of Mark's hearers or the mind of Jesus? Not necessarily. Mark cites a dramatic warning of Jesus in Mark 8–10, the section where he applies Jesus' teachings to what it means to live in Christian community. "If any of you put a stumbling-block before one of these little ones who believe in me, it would be better for you if a great millstone were hung around your neck and you were thrown into the sea" (9:42). It is the first of a series of shocking sayings attributed to Jesus. They include that people should cut off their hands or feet and pluck out their eyes if they cause people to stumble (9:43–48). These are violent images designed to stop people in their tracks and make them think.

Matthew also copies Mark at this point (Matt 18:6–9), enhancing the severity of the warning by inserting, before the warning about excising hands, the comment: "Woe to the world because of stumbling-blocks! Occasions for stumbling are bound to come, but woe to the one by whom the stumbling-block comes!" (18:7). Matthew had already included sayings about excision in the Sermon on the Mount. There they supplement Jesus' warning about adulterous desire and looking after another man's wife (5:28). "If your right eye causes you to sin, tear it out and throw it away; it is better for you to lose one of your members than for your whole body to be thrown into hell. And if your right hand causes you to sin, cut it off and throw it away; it is better for you to lose one of your members than for your whole body to go into hell" (Matt 5:29–30). These warnings in Matthew are about sexual wrongdoing. That is very likely to be the way people listening to Matthew's Gospel would have heard them when they were repeated a second time in 18:8–9. A sexual connotation is not explicit in Mark's account but may be implied. The shocking form of the statements was saying: take sexual wrongdoing seriously. The language of stumbling or causing others to stumble was, indeed, sometimes used of sexual wrongdoing. The Greek word, *skandalon*, comes through in English as scandal. It appears throughout Mark 9:42–47.

When, therefore, Mark begins with the warning, "If any of you put a stumbling-block before one of these little ones who believe in me, it would be better for you if a great millstone were hung around your neck and you were thrown into the sea" (9:42), it is likely that a sexual connotation is present. While it is possible that "these little ones who believe in me" might simply be a term for believers of any age, it is more likely that it refers to children "These little ones who believe in me" would refer to children in the Christian community. That is made more probable in the light of what comes just a few verses earlier in Mark where he has Jesus confront the ambitions of the disciples to be important: "he took a little child and put it among them; and taking it in his arms, he said to them, 'Whoever welcomes one such child in my name welcomes me, and whoever welcomes me welcomes not me but the one who sent me'" (Mark 9:36–37).

Matthew has Jesus warn about causing a child to "stumble" immediately after bringing the child before them.

> At that time the disciples came to Jesus and asked, "Who is the greatest in the kingdom of heaven?" He called a child, whom he put among them, and said, "Truly I tell you, unless you change and become like children, you will never enter the kingdom of heaven. Whoever becomes humble like this child is the greatest in the kingdom of heaven. Whoever welcomes one such child in my name welcomes me." (Matt 18:1–5)

In Matthew the warning may now refer to any believer, but it seems possible that there was a memory preserved in these texts of Jesus' warning against child abuse. Pedophilia, common in the ancient world, was to have no place in the community.

Pedophilia is not to be confused with same-gender sexual orientation, as sometimes occurs. Pedophilia is sexual abuse of minors, whatever their gender. So Jesus' warning may only by extension be applied to potential male abuse of male minors, an issue of his time, especially in the wider world.

## More Allusions?

Are there further potential references to same-gender sexual relations in the New Testament outside of Paul? When the Book of Revelation refers to those excluded from the new Jerusalem, it declares: "Outside are the dogs and sorcerers and fornicators and murderers and idolaters, and everyone who loves and practices falsehood" (Rev 22:15). "Dogs" here may refer to male prostitutes, as possibly in Deut 23:17–18, or to men actively engaging in anal penetration.

We also find references to Sodom and Gomorrah as instances of where God's judgement was exercised. "Likewise, Sodom and Gomorrah and the surrounding cities, which, in the same manner as they, indulged in sexual immorality and pursued unnatural lust [literally: went after other flesh], serve as an example by undergoing a punishment of eternal fire" (Jude 7). The author had already cited God's anger with the wilderness generation and with the wayward Watchers. "In the same manner as they" refers to the Watchers. They transgressed by having sexual intercourse with women. In what way did the men of Sodom and Gomorrah act similarly? The text suggests that they "went after other flesh." That might refer to sexual promiscuity generally. "Other" could mean "other" than women, but that is unclear. Alternatively, it would refer to their wanting to rape the angels, the Watchers, just mentioned. It would in any case imply a reference to male rape.

In rewriting parts of Jude, 2 Peter again refers to Sodom and Gomorrah as an example of God's judgement along with the

Watchers and Noah's generation but offers little about their sin (2 Pet 2:4–10). The allusion to Sodom and Gomorrah in Matt 10:14–15 and Luke 10:10–12 focuses on their lack of hospitality, not on their sexual behavior as such, and threatens even greater judgement on those not offering hospitality to Jesus' envoys.

## Jesus on Same-Gender Sex?

We have no evidence of Jesus ever addressing issues of same-gender sex, except possibly in the stark comment warning about child abuse. He cites Genesis 1:27 about God making male and female and Genesis 2:24 on marriage as two becoming flesh in order to assert the permanency of marriage in the context of prohibiting divorce (Mark 10:2–12). He was not doing so, however, in order to deal with alternatives such as gay marriage and gay sexual relationships.

If we probe the dark and speculate into the silence, we would have to say that, if Jesus were asked, we would expect that he would almost certainly have shared the assumptions of his time based on Genesis 1:27—that all people were either male or female and were heterosexual—and taken the strict line that we have noted in all surviving Jewish literature from his era, namely that to have sex with someone of the same gender was sin. It was sin because it was to act contrary to one's created nature. On matters sexual he was one with John the Baptist in taking a very strict line in condemning Herod Antipas for incest in marrying the divorced wife of his brother-in-law (Mark 6:17–18), something no longer deemed as incest in most legislatures.

Jesus was, of course, dependent on the science and understanding of his time and this should be respected. Just because, for instance, he would have shared with his contemporaries the belief that the world was flat or, had he known Greek theories, that the sun revolved around the earth, does not render his gospel in any way invalid. Faith does not entail believing that Jesus wandered about Galilee with an internal hard drive, as it were, complete with advanced scientific knowledge, even beyond ours, and just kept quiet about it. If we again probe the dark and speculate about what Jesus or Paul might say *today*, having learned that the world is not flat and that not all people are heterosexual, what might we say? Given their form in not following a fundamentalist literalism but adapting to what is most caring, as with Paul and others on circumcision and food laws, what is likely? Surely the same love and flexibility.

## Eunuchs and Celibacy

If the passages discussed above relate mainly abusive forms of same-gender sexual relations and the abuse of minors, are there any other indications of awareness of LGBTQI+ people in the New Testament aside from the obvious references in Paul's writings? In the previous chapter we mentioned eunuchs. The Book of Acts refers to an Ethiopian eunuch, converted to faith in Jesus by Philip. He is described as "a court official of the Candace, queen of the Ethiopians" (Acts 8:27). He may be literally a eunuch, an impotent male, or he may be simply an official. Nothing in the story tells us more than that.

There is, however, another reference to eunuchs in a saying attributed to Jesus in response to his disciples' reaction to his strict teaching about divorce, musing that it is perhaps better not to get married at all.

> His disciples said to him, "If such is the case of a man with his wife, it is better not to marry." But he said to them, "Not everyone can accept this teaching, but only those to whom it is given. For there are eunuchs who have been so from birth, and there are eunuchs who have been made eunuchs by others, and there are eunuchs who have made themselves eunuchs for the sake of the kingdom of heaven. Let anyone accept this who can." (Matt 19:10–12)

As noted in the previous chapter, the assumption was that some men are born impotent—not able to propagate—and some are made that way through castration. Castration was sometimes an act of subjugation and humiliation in war, but it could also be a means of control, especially of slaves and subordinates. It rendered them safe from the perspective of their owners in positions where they had responsibility involving women, such as in royal courts and harems. It did not rob them of their sexual desire, but they could not make women pregnant. They might not engage in sexual activity at all, but they were sometimes notorious for sexual engagement with women manually or with men in a passive role. Accordingly, they sometimes had a bad reputation, or were at least looked down upon as men because of their impotence, and especially when they took a passive role in sexual encounters with men. Eunuchs were not seen as gay men, but as males without reproductive potential. Some have wondered if by "eunuchs from birth" the saying in Matthew 19:12 is referring to intersex people, sometimes in later traditions also called eunuchs, but the focus in the context is on not being able to reproduce, not something impossible for intersex people. In that sense, the reference to eunuchs here adds nothing to our stock of allusions to same-gender sexual relationships in the New Testament.

The saying of Jesus refers to voluntary eunuchs. This was a way of referring to men who felt called to live celibate lives, that is, to remain or become unmarried and not to engage sexually at all. Some saw this as a way of being more available to fulfil their calling. Some related it to purity concerns in the sense that engagement in sexual intercourse rendered a person in need of ritual cleansing before entering sacred space. That applied to the temple, but it could also be seen as applying to those constantly engaged in closeness to God, such as prophets, and generally to times that people set aside for prayers. Paul reflects this belief when he writes of couples abstaining from sexual intercourse for the sake of prayer (1 Cor 7:5). He then adds that they should then go back to meeting each other's sexual needs in sexual engagement, with a warning that not to do so might have Satan create in them a desire to meet their sexual needs in illegitimate ways. In the previous chapter he had warned about involvement in such illicit relations, probably referring to prostitution.

Paul believed he was living in the last days and would, in his lifetime, see Jesus return. In addition, he believed that the age to come would be one characterized by sacred space and so having no place for sex and marriage. Mark reports Jesus as saying something similar: "For when they rise from the dead, they neither marry nor are given in marriage, but are like angels in heaven" (Mark 2:25). Accordingly, some saw themselves called to live in the present the way they would live in the future. That had been Paul's choice and he recommended it to others. It lies behind his statement at the beginning of 1 Corinthians 7, that it was good for a man not to touch (i.e., have sexual relations with) a woman. For the same reason, he also advised slaves against trying to change their status. Time is too short.

In saying this about sexual intercourse he had, however, to tread carefully because some in Corinth were taking it a step further and demanding that all live like that. Paul, therefore, had to balance his own preference on the one hand—which they wanted to generalize and apply to everyone, and his belief that marriage and sexual relations in marriage in this age and era were part of the good order of creation. He insists more than once that people marrying and having sex were not sinning (1 Cor 7:9, 28, 36). Celibacy is not for all. He put it this way: "I wish that all were as I myself am. But each has a particular gift from God, one having one kind and another a different kind. To the unmarried and the widows I say that it is well for them to remain unmarried as I am. But if they are not practicing self-control, they should marry. For it is better to marry than to be aflame with passion" (1 Cor 7:7–9).

The issue must have come up also in Matthew's community in relation to Jesus choosing celibacy, because Matthew has Jesus declare: "Not everyone can accept this teaching, but only those to whom it is given" (Matt 19:10). Celibacy is not for everyone, and celibates are not superiors. The Book of Revelation reflects acceptance of both options when it symbolically writes of 144,000: "It is these who have not [ritually] defiled themselves with women, for they are virgins" (Rev 14:4). An earlier chapter depicts them being joined by myriads of others: "After this I looked, and there was a great multitude that no one could count, from every nation, from all tribes and peoples and languages, standing before the throne and before the Lamb, robed in white, with palm branches in their hands" (Rev 7:9). They would from then on also be celibate in heaven's holy space.

Neither eunuchs nor celibates have any bearing on the issue of same-gender sexual relations in the New Testament. Those whose approach to Scripture see it not as *human witness to God*, through which God speaks, and in that sense the Word of God, but treat it as more than human, that is, as *God's own words* and so infallible, sometimes try very hard to find in it what fits their own belief systems. Some even try to find reference to the earth being round and in orbit around the sun. Similar concern among those who affirm same-gender sexual orientation as a fact of life often searches also for signs of its acceptance.

## The Beloved Disciple

We noted the endeavor to search for possible traces of positive attitudes towards same-gender sexual relations in the case of David and Jonathan in discussing the Old Testament. If only we could show it was a gay relationship, then we could be happy that the Bible says gay relationships are acceptable. This is a false move framed on a very inadequate understanding of what the Bible is.

Nevertheless, some have wondered whether the reference to "the disciple whom Jesus loved" in the New Testament provides such support. Did Jesus have a homoerotic relationship with one of his disciples, the beloved disciple? This figure appears only in the Gospel according to John. The author probably wanted us to identify him as the disciple, John. Was he, indeed, Jesus' gay lover? If not, why is he singled out in this way? The author certainly depicts him as very special. He outruns Peter to the tomb (20:4). He has the inside running in relation to the high priest and his inner circle (18:15–17). He reclines next to Jesus, literally by his chest, during his last meal and becomes the conduit for Peter's question about Jesus' betrayer (13:25). Being that close recalls the words about Jesus being so close to the Father in 1:18. He is entrusted by Jesus with care of his mother (19:26–27). He was the subject of rumor that he might survive until Jesus' return (21:20–23). He is the major source and inspiration for the very different depiction of Jesus in John's Gospel (21:24–24).

Is the beloved disciple, then, the model of a loving gay relationship in which Jesus was engaged? Were both of them gay men, providing a model for all such relationships in the future, not something abusive, but something beautiful? I can appreciate how helpful such a notion might be. The image rests on speculation in the silence, probings in the dark. Is it likely? The evidence suggests it is not. There is an absence of any sexual allusions. That is not in itself necessarily a problem, since close gay relationships need not always be seen through a sexualized lens or be sexual. It is a problem, however, that subsequent hearers and readers did not see it so, especially where all such relationships were deemed abominable. Nor do we see signs of sensitivity to the possibility that the relationship could be understood in this way and so of any undertakings to correct such an impression.

Indeed, what we see in the very creative and powerful depiction of Jesus in John's Gospel is a trend that was evident in second-century gospels. There we see them implying or explicitly claiming that their inspiration came from secret information given through Jesus' special friendship with one of the disciples. Mary Magdalene is an example in the Gospel of Mary. Not yet Jesus' lover and wife, as in some later texts and fantasies, she appears as one to whom Jesus imparted secret revelations now disclosed in the gospel attributed to her. Similar claims are made of secret revelation given to Thomas, and even to Judas Iscariot. People were aware of such literary techniques employed to give special status to their portraits.

The church, with only some dissent, saw in the Gospel according to John, a faithful portrait of the essence of Jesus' message, capturing his significance not in conclusions and commentaries, but in almost every scene, as bearer of God's light and life. They recognized its distinctive style and creativity, sometimes calling it the "spiritual gospel." The beloved disciple is probably based on a figure of the past reworked to serve the image. This is more likely than that he was Jesus' otherwise forgotten or neglected partner in love.

There is, therefore, very little in the New Testament outside of Paul, that has to do with same-gender sexual relations. The only possible exception is Jesus' stern warning about abuse of little ones, targeting pedophilia. It is not that sexual matters never arose. They are nearly always present, directly or indirectly, because they are part of what it means to be human. Where we find most references to sexual matters is in the writings associated with Paul. We turn to these in the next two chapters.

6

# The Writings of Paul
# Outside of Romans

DISCUSSIONS OF HOMOSEXUALITY IN the New Testament have basically one main text, the first chapter of Paul's letter to the Romans. We devote the next chapter solely to that passage. While it makes good sense to put the focus there, it is also important to note that the writings in which he makes most reference to sexual matters are his letters to the Corinthians. Indeed, almost all the correspondence exchanged with the Corinthians, his letters to them and their letters to him, contain reference to sexual matters.

## Sexuality Matters

This should not surprise us. As noted in the conclusion to the previous chapter, our sexuality is an important aspect of our being human. It is not something peripheral or an optional extra able to be given attention at will. It is right there in our brain, our most important sexual organ, and in our emotions, our physical and psychological self. Any discussion of these is bound at some stage to address it. For Paul as a good Jew, sexuality was part of how

God made us and so was to be handled with care and attention. As a good Jew of his time, educated within a world open also to the wisdom of the lifestyle philosophies of well-being, he also knew that part of handling one's sexuality with care meant keeping it under control and not going to excess, quite apart from the overall principle of seeking to live in harmony with nature, understood in a Jewish context as one's created nature.

He would have shared the widespread recognition that how one handled sexuality was important not only for one's own health, but also for the health of others and not least of the household. Don't do anything that would destabilize or damage yourself or your household. He would have shared these concerns not only with fellow Jews but also with thinking men and women in the wider community beyond his Jewish community. Sex mattered. Emperors gave edicts to keep it in control—from prosecution of adultery to encouragement to men to marry earlier in their twenties, a wise move that would help them and help society to reduce the excesses of the wild stallions that some became, as they sometimes put it.

There was another dimension to Paul's concerns. He was part of a Jewish movement meeting in house groups, not as connected families but as a religious group having its origin in the east, being spread by followers of Jesus. Jews were already viewed by many outsiders as a little odd in their observances of Sabbath, food laws, and the like. They had been around for a long time and that was tolerable. They could even serve in armies and make other contributions to society. They represented ancient tradition in an age when the old was held in high regard and the new treated with suspicion. This new group, however, seemed to be a mixture of Jews and others. Thus, its status was ambiguous.

Just being a new group would have brought this new Jewish movement under suspicion. It was, therefore, all the more important that they not do anything that would add to that suspicion. That continued to be a concern the more the movement spread. Those who, with great respect, wrote with Paul's name and authority the letters to the Colossians and the Ephesians emphasized how important it was that members of the movement upheld household values. These included that husbands and wives behave accordingly: the man, the leader, the wife, his subordinate helper, the children, taught obedience and not abused, and the slaves, obedient to the household master and not being abused by him. Later writings—some also penned as Paul's, others as penned by Peter—reinforced the need for such household order, not least so as to present a respectable form to the wider community with its concerns.

Such instruction could easily have been drawn from any set of guidelines for proper households in the wider world of the time and tweaked to reflect the movement's values. Love such as Christ showed for the church was to characterize the husband's treatment of his wife (Eph 5:25–33). The same love also shapes the way the other pairings—parent-child and master-slave—are discussed. Much is left unsaid, particularly about sexual behavior and what was and was not forbidden within such relationships. We may assume that normal Jewish values would have been determinative, including sexual fidelity in marriage, prohibition of incest and sexual exploitation of minors. Were slaves still deemed sexually accessible to masters? The matter is not addressed.

These small religious communities, which began to multiply across the empire's cities, would later face charges that they were cannibals who gathered to eat human flesh and drink human blood and do so in the context of love feasts that left little to the imagination. A truly dangerous sect! A truly disturbing misunderstanding!

## Incest at Corinth

In Paul's correspondence with the Corinthians there are different matters. The first to be addressed was the case of a man sleeping with his father's wife (1 Cor 5:1–2). This will have been his father's second wife. His own mother was the first. She might have given birth to him some fifteen or so years before and, like many women, did not survive beyond around thirty. We have then a teenage boy from that first marriage and his father with a new wife—perhaps even the same age as the boy. It must have happened quite often that the two, a teenage boy and his step-mother, became sexually attracted.

Of course, it was not acceptable, neither in Jewish society nor in the wider world. Paul is outraged and writes: "It is actually reported that there is sexual immorality among you, and of a kind that is not found even among pagans; for a man is living with his father's wife" (1 Cor 5:1). It probably did happen among pagans, but Paul was right in his observation that it was also not acceptable there.

The man is to be banished from the group. Paul scolds the group for not acting sooner. Earlier in the letter he mentions that visitors from Corinth had been reporting abuses in the congregation (1 Cor 1:11). Having challenged them to act in relation to this case of incest he then mentions a previous letter he had written, which has not survived. "I wrote to you in my letter not to associate with sexually immoral persons—not at all meaning the immoral of this world, or the greedy and robbers, or idolaters, since you would then need to go out of the world. But now I am writing to you not to associate with anyone who bears the name of brother or sister who is sexually immoral or greedy, or is an idolater, reviler, drunkard, or robber. Do not even eat with such a one" (1 Cor 5:9–11). Internal discipline was vital for such communities. The movement had its beginnings, and continued to have its values, based on a generosity that reached out to all kinds of sinners, but that never should mean tolerating such sin within the community itself.

Paul goes on to criticize those who, it had been reported, were taking other believers to court before secular judges. He urged them not to do so, but to deal with conflicts internally. This advice has had an unfortunate legacy right through to recent times when churches often failed to report sexual abuse to civil authorities.

## "Male-Bedders" and "Softies"

Paul continues by reminding them that there should be no place in their house groups for people engaging in sinful practices because, ultimately, they have no place in God's kingdom:

> Do you not know that wrongdoers will not inherit the kingdom of God? Do not be deceived! The sexually immoral, idolaters, adulterers, softies, male bedders, thieves, the greedy, drunkards, revilers, robbers—none of these will inherit the kingdom of God. And this is what some of you used to be. But you were washed, you were sanctified, you were justified in the name of the Lord Jesus Christ and in the Spirit of our God. (1 Cor 6:9–11)

I have slightly modified the NRSV translation of this passage in the interests of greater accuracy and clarity. I have replaced "fornicators" (quaint and rarely in use in contemporary English) with "the sexually immoral." The Greek word that it translates, *pornoi*, had come to mean anyone engaged in sexual wrongdoing. The Greek translation of the Ten Commandments lists the commandment not to commit adultery as the first on the second of the two stone tablets given to Moses, ahead of murder and stealing. It is, accordingly, quite common to begin lists of wrongdoing with sexual wrongdoing. The commandment not to commit adultery became a kind of heading under which to include all acts of sexual wrongdoing.

Much more significant are changes of "male prostitutes" and "sodomites" to "softies" and "male-bedders." I translate the Greek word *arsenokoitai* literally as "male-bedders." *Arseno* means male and *koitai* come from the word for bed, reflected also in the word coitus. Paul's use of it here is the first we know of. It is clearly about males and beds. It is about sexual behavior, but it hardly means males who go to bed with people, who could be men or women, but is better understood as men who bed males. As such it refers to the active partner in same-gender sexual relations. It may well have been created on the basis of the prohibitions in Leviticus, which also make reference to males and beds and in the Greek use similar wording.

The word that immediately precedes is *malakoi* and means literally "soft ones." There is nothing to suggest it implies "prostitute." That is more an interpretation than a translation. *Malakos* is the word for soft. It is not a *technical* term for the passive partner in a sexual encounter between men. It was used of effeminate men and so, in all probability, refers here to the passive partners in a same-gender sexual relationship.

Paul may be using a standard list of who are sinners, or it may be his own. Its contents reflect standard understandings of what constituted sin among his fellow Jews and members of his movement. Reference to those engaging in homosexual acts is simply listed alongside a range of other sinners and not given any attention beyond that. We find a similar list of sins in Galatians, but without reference to people engaged in same-gender sex:

> Now the works of the flesh are obvious: fornication, impurity, licentiousness, idolatry, sorcery, enmities, strife, jealousy, anger, quarrels, dissensions, factions, envy, drunkenness, carousing, and things like these. I am warning you, as I warned you before: those who do such things will not inherit the kingdom of God. (Gal 5:19–21)

In 1 Timothy, a writing penned in Paul's name and so perpetuating his teaching and concerns, we have a similar list.

> Now we know that the law is good, if one uses it legitimately. This means understanding that the law is laid down not for the innocent but for the lawless and disobedient, for the godless and sinful, for the unholy and profane, for those who kill their father or mother, for murderers, the sexually immoral, male bedders, slave-traders, liars, perjurers, and whatever else is contrary to the sound teaching that conforms to the glorious gospel of the blessed God, which he entrusted to me. (1 Tim 1:8–11)

Again, I have replaced the NRSV's quaint "fornicators" with "the sexually immoral" and "sodomites" with "male-bedders." In translating *arsenokoitai* by sodomites the NRSV is more correct than in 1 Cor 6:9 because "sodomites" refers to the active partner. The fact that immediately following the reference to active partners in same-gender sex we have reference to slave traders, may be significant. One aspect of the slave trade was buying slaves for sexual exploitation.

Both lists offer little more than categories of whose practices should not be tolerated in the believing community and offer no further comment beyond that. It may well be that the word "male-bedders" had connotations of exploitation and violence. This may be why it comes immediately before reference to slave traders in 1 Timothy. Later uses of the word sometimes occur in contexts of violence and exploitation, but the word was probably not limited to that. *Malakoi* is perhaps more indicative of consent. As we have seen in other instances, to go beyond the text is to grope in the dark and speculate in the silence.

## Illicit Sex with Women

If the references to men engaging in homosexual acts are somewhat incidental in Paul's statement in 1 Cor 6:9–11, the references that follow in warnings against sexual wrongdoing are much more explicit.

> "All things are lawful for me," but not all things are beneficial. "All things are lawful for me," but I will not be dominated by anything. "Food is meant for the stomach and the stomach for food," and God will destroy both one and the other. The body is meant not for fornication [sexual immorality] but for the Lord, and the Lord for the body. (1 Cor 6:12–13)

The statements, "All things are lawful for me" and "All things are lawful for me," may, as the NRSV translation suggests, be quotations. Was Paul citing something the Corinthians had written in their letter, referred to in 7:1 ("concerning the matters about which you wrote")? Or was he citing himself from a previous occasion? These words would certainly sit well with some of his statements elsewhere. His concern is to qualify them not to reject them. He shifts the focus, however, away from what one is freed *from* to what one is freed *for*. How does one exercise the freedom that had been given believers through Christ?

Did it matter? It certainly did! Not only was there an issue of whether one's behavior was beneficial or harmful, but also whether it led to a new captivity. Don't let yourself be dominated, is Paul's message. This fitted the standard ideal for the Roman male, which was not to be dominated, but it also fitted Paul's notion of healthy humanity. Being dominated by one's desire for food was an obvious danger, at least to oneself. Paul, however, mentions that simply as a steppingstone towards talking about sexual desire. Don't be dominated by it. More specifically, don't let yourself, your body, be dominated by it. Submit yourself to the Lord.

Paul consistently spoke not of freedom to do what you like but freedom to enter a relationship with Christ. Accordingly, he argues:

> Do you not know that your bodies are members of Christ? Should I therefore take the members of Christ and make them members of a prostitute? Never! Do you not know that whoever is united to a prostitute becomes one body with her? For it is said, "The two shall be one flesh." (1 Cor 6:15–16)

The word translated "prostitute" here is *porne*, such as we find in the word pornography. From being a word for prostitute, it had become a term for any immoral woman, just as the word *porneia*, originally a reference to prostitution, had become a standard word for sexual wrongdoing. We cannot therefore immediately assume that Paul is speaking of Corinthians going to prostitutes. On the other hand, the reference later in 6:20 to a price suggests that "prostitute" may well be the meaning here.

It is striking that Paul cites Genesis 2:24, used elsewhere to explain the origin of marriage after God made Eve from Adam: "Therefore a man leaves his father and his mother and clings to his wife, and they become one flesh." Sexual intercourse creates a bond. This is the assumption. You cannot have a bond with a prostitute *and* a bond with Christ. That is the argument. It connects to the concern not to be dominated by another.

Paul sees sex with a prostitute not as a one-off act but as an event that makes people one. It changes them. For this reason, he goes on to write: "But anyone united to the Lord becomes one spirit with him. Shun fornication [sexual wrongdoing]! Every sin that a person commits is outside the body; but the fornicator [one engaging in sexual wrongdoing] sins against the body itself" (1

Cor 6:17–18). Paul argues that sin through sexual intercourse with a prostitute is not like stealing or murder because it has an impact on your whole person. It is a sin against yourself. The implications are clear. You cannot be one body with both a prostitute and Christ. Paul reinforces his claim: "Or do you not know that your body is a temple of the Holy Spirit within you, which you have from God, and that you are not your own? For you were bought with a price; therefore glorify God in your body" (1 Cor 6:19–20). The play on Christ's death as like a payment to redeem a slave or captive is probably deliberate in order to make a contrast with payment to a prostitute.

Paul's concerns with sexual wrongdoing at Corinth did not go away. In 2 Corinthians he writes: "I fear that when I come again, my God may humble me before you, and that I may have to mourn over many who previously sinned and have not repented of the impurity, sexual immorality, and licentiousness that they have practiced" (2 Cor 13:21). Paul expresses his concern primarily in relation to the man. Sadly, he gives no attention to what it might mean for the woman. His argument could produce confusion, especially if read as also meaning that a man should not have sexual intercourse with his wife, as though being one with even one's own wife means you cannot be one with Christ. That was clearly not Paul's view. He saw marriage between believers who were part of the corporate body of Christ as being perfectly acceptable, because both own Christ as Lord and belong in the one body. This is very clear in what he then goes on to address.

## Preferring Celibacy but Defending Marriage

As noted in the previous chapter, Paul's expectation was that Christ would come back during his lifetime (e.g., 1 Thess 4:15; 1 Cor 15:51–52) and that the age to come would be one where marriage and sexual relations would have no place, it being a sacred place and life of a different order. His initial statement in 1 Corinthians 7 reflects these assumptions: "Now concerning the matters about which you wrote: 'It is well for a man not to touch a woman'"

(7:1). It is not clear whether the statement about not touching a woman, a common euphemism for having sex, is something that was in the Corinthians' letter or something that Paul was saying, in which case it should not be translated as a quotation. It is certainly something like the statements in 6:12 about all things being lawful with which Paul agreed but needed to qualify.

Whether his own words or theirs, the statement about it being better not to have sex with women would reflect Paul's view as he understood it and which he then clarified in what follows.

> But because of cases of sexual immorality, each man should have his own wife and each woman her own husband. The husband should give to his wife her conjugal rights, and likewise the wife to her husband. For the wife does not have authority over her own body, but the husband does; likewise the husband does not have authority over his own body, but the wife does. (1 Cor 7:2–4)

This statement has given Paul a bad press, as though he saw marriage only as a mechanism to protect people from sexual immorality and nothing more. Clearly, he understood marriage as more than that and could later write of each seeking the interests of the other (7:32–34). The focus of his statement is mutuality, even expressed not as the wife being subject to the husband but each being subject to each other, including meeting each other's sexual needs. There is a connection between this statement and what Paul had said about being under another's authority in the previous chapter. Being subject to one another when both are subject to Christ is his model. While not marriage's only purpose, marriage does help deal with unsatisfied sexual desire, in response to which some were apparently visiting prostitutes.

Paul's urging that partners meet each other's needs could be read in such a way as would make it acceptable for one partner to force their needs on the other, such as occurs in marital rape. This would not be in keeping with what Paul writes here and elsewhere.

Paul goes on to urge again that they meet each other's needs: "Do not deprive one another, except perhaps by agreement for a set time, to devote yourselves to prayer, and then come together again, so that Satan may not tempt you because of your lack of self-control. This I say by way of concession, not of command" (1 Cor 7:5–6). What he concedes is not that they may engage in sexual intercourse, but the opposite. They can abstain for purposes of prayer.

As noted above, this connects to his assumption, one commonly held, that sacred space and time should be free of acts that would make one ritually impure and so disqualified to be in sacred space. He is conceding that it is acceptable to withhold from having sexual intercourse under those circumstances, but urges that such abstention should be limited. Otherwise, he fears, some may respond to having unfulfilled sexual desire and go off to prostitutes. Was Paul being overly pessimistic or just realistic? Probably realistic, given what we know of cultural norms in Corinth, which had a reputation for sexual promiscuity.

Paul affirms marriage against those who might have concluded that all should live now the way they will be living in the world to come, namely in celibacy, and so should leave their marriages. He does not hide the fact that celibacy is the option he has chosen but underlines that this was not something he expected of everyone. He was certainly not wanting to encourage Corinthians to abandon their marriages as, it seems, some were inclined to do.

## To Marry or Not to Marry?

In what follows he addresses the implications of what he has been saying, first addressing the unmarried: "To the unmarried and the widows I say that it is well for them to remain unmarried as I am. But if they are not practicing self-control, they should marry. For it is better to marry than to be aflame with passion" (1 Cor 7:8–9). Paul is a realist. Some people find celibacy easy. Some do not. They should not feel guilty about that. They should marry, Paul's assumption being, of course, that having sexual intercourse before marrying was inappropriate, at the very least, because it could result in one's partner becoming pregnant while unmarried, something deemed very shameful. Paul is not implying that to have strong passion and to marry for this reason is sin. Passion is part of how God made us. It all depends on how one responds to it.

In addressing married people, he can draw on the strict saying of Jesus about divorce: "To the married I give this command—not I but the Lord—that the wife should not separate from her husband (but if she does separate, let her remain unmarried or else be reconciled to her husband), and that the husband should not divorce his wife" (1 Cor 7:10–11). He probably assumes what Matthew makes explicit, that, of course, divorce becomes mandatory where adultery has taken place. Normally in Jewish culture husbands divorced wives, not vice versa, but a woman could leave her husband, effectively divorcing him. Perhaps Paul has heard of a woman taking the initiative to separate from her husband and this is why he speaks of a woman. The words in brackets are probably his interpretation, urging that she should go back, or at least remain unmarried. Some probably treated Jesus' words as unchangeable law, but Paul now found himself in a situation that required flexibility and imagination.

What if one partner joins the church and the other does not? Was it thinkable that only one half of the one body—the one flesh that they had become—was within the body of Christ and the other half was not? Paul's solution is practical. If the unbelieving partner wants to stay, let it be, he advises, and if they want to go, let that be, too. Accept the divorce and feel free to remarry. If they stay, Paul muses, there will be an impact on the other and on their children from the believing partner being in holy space. It sounds almost magical to modern ears, but people those days thought of holiness as like an influence that could affect those around you, quite apart from going further to contemplate that the partner might finally be won over to the faith.

Paul's underlying concern for the wellbeing of people and the church enabled him to adapt what seemed an inflexible prohibition of Jesus. In this, he was following a tradition of interpreting and applying Scripture and the words of Jesus not as inflexible law but as something to be seen in the light of the greater command of love and applied flexibly in new situations.

Paul had been criticized for doing so when he chose to work part time to support his ministry instead of sticking to Jesus' command that envoys not work but expect locals to support them. In 1 Corinthians 9 he defends his position. It was all about being flexible and realistic and doing what best cohered with the love that is at the heart of the gospel. The same perspective had enabled the church to set the requirement of circumcision aside and the rules about clean and unclean foods, despite the turbulence that ensued from those more inclined to a fundamentalist approach.

Indeed, Paul goes on to cite circumcision as an example, but more to say that, despite those demanding otherwise, they should stay as they are, uncircumcised. Partly this was also because he saw no point, given the shortness of time, of making major changes. That informed then his advice to slaves not to seek their freedom but claim the different kind of freedom they have in Christ, to whom they now owe loyalty. Taken out of context, Paul's advice that slaves remain slaves put a brake on changes that took eighteen centuries to achieve and still need to be fought for.

Paul returns to marriage in 7:25–31, discussing young women who were still virgins and men not yet married or engaged to be married. Given his assumptions, it makes sense that his advice to them is not to go ahead, but, as in his advice to the widowed, he makes it very clear that if they do go ahead, it is not a sin (7:28). In the light of the fact that the last days are upon them, minimizing stress and anxiety should be the priority. He assumes the married face greater stress.

The NRSV translation then reads as though Paul is again addressing engaged people in 7:36–38 because it translates a Greek word usually meaning "give away in marriage" simply as "marry." It is more likely that Paul is addressing fathers about how they should manage their unmarried daughters. Again, Paul sets out his preferences: better not to have them marry, but if they do, take comfort in the fact that this is not sin. It might then better read in translation as follows:

> If anyone thinks that he is not behaving properly towards
> his virgin [daughter], if she has reached sexual maturity,

and so it has to be, let him do as he wishes; it is no sin. Let them [the couple] marry. But if someone stands firm in his resolve, being under no necessity but being in control of what he wants to do, and has determined in his own mind to keep her [unmarried] as his virgin daughter, he will do well. So then, he who gives away his virgin daughter in marriage does well; and he who refrains from giving her away in marriage will do better. (1 Cor 7:36–38)

## Marrying Only "in the Lord"

Paul's final words are about widows, assuring them of their freedom to remarry, but with the proviso that it be "in the Lord," that is, to a fellow believer.

Concern about intermarriage with non-Jews had been a major concern among many Jewish writers, as we noted. This stance remained a concern within the early Christian movement, but now was redefined in terms of opposition to mixed marriages with unbelievers. That is why Paul stipulates that widows may remarry, but must marry "in the Lord."

The issue reappears in 2 Corinthians, where Paul insists on believers not marrying unbelievers.

Do not be mismatched with unbelievers. For what partnership is there between righteousness and lawlessness? Or what fellowship is there between light and darkness? What agreement does Christ have with Beliar? Or what does a believer share with an unbeliever? What agreement has the temple of God with idols? (2 Cor 6:14–16)

The word translated "mismatched" means literally "be unevenly yoked." To be yoked with someone was a common term for being married to someone. Paul's language here is very strong, and he backs it up with a mix of biblical quotations. I give the sources in brackets:

I will live in them and walk among them [Lev 26:11–12],
and I will be their God, and they shall be my people [Ezek

37:27]. Therefore come out from them, and be separate from them, says the Lord, and touch nothing unclean [Isa 52:11]; then I will welcome you [Ezek 20:34], and I will be your father, and you shall be my sons and daughters, says the Lord Almighty [2 Sam 7:8]. (2 Cor 6:16–18)

Paul may well have borrowed this patchwork of biblical citations from a Jewish source concerned with intermarriage, if he did not weave it together himself. It now applies to the believing community of followers of Jesus who see themselves as holy.

He may also have been alluding indirectly to the issue of intermarriage in 1 Corinthians 10 when he cites examples of God's judgement against Israel for its disobedience: "Now these things occurred as examples for us, so that we might not desire evil as they did. Do not become idolaters as some of them did; as it is written, 'The people sat down to eat and drink, and they rose up to play.' We must not indulge in sexual immorality as some of them did, and twenty-three thousand fell in a single day" (1 Cor 10:6–8). According to Numbers 25 some Israelite men had sexual relations with Moabite women who invited them to participate in idolatrous practices. As a result, God sent a plague, killing twenty-four thousand in a single day (Num 25:1–9). The discrepancy in the numbers between twenty-three and twenty-four thousand may be the result of confusion with Numbers 26:62, which mentions twenty-three thousand of the descendants of Levi's sons not listed. Paul's primary concern in the chapter, however, is the Corinthians' possible connections with idol worship: "Therefore, my dear friends, flee from the worship of idols" (1 Cor 10:14).

Like the author of the Book of Wisdom, Paul saw a connection between people having distorted ideas of God, idolatry, and having distorted understanding of themselves and so behaving in sexually immoral ways. Already in writing to the Thessalonians Paul makes that connection:

> For this is the will of God, your sanctification: that you abstain from fornication; that each one of you knows how to control your own body in holiness and honor, not with lustful passion, like the Gentiles who do not know

God; that no one wrongs or exploits a brother or sister in this matter, because the Lord is an avenger in all these things, just as we have already told you beforehand and solemnly warned you. For God did not call us to impurity but in holiness. (1 Thess 4:3–7)

"Gentiles who do not know God" engage in sexual wrongdoing as a result. The Greek speaks of wronging not "a brother or sister," but simply "a brother," so that some have wondered if it might refer to a man sexually exploiting another man. It is much more likely to refer to a man wronging another man by engaging in adultery with his wife—in effect, an act of theft. The translation, "a brother or sister," seeks to be inclusive in its language, but obscures the meaning.

Have a perverted relationship with God and you will have a perverted relationship with yourself. Paul elaborates this theme more fully in Romans 1 in his depiction of same-gender sexual relations as typifying of the world's depravity. To this we turn in the following chapter.

# 7

# Paul in Romans

"LET'S HEAD FOR SPAIN, stopping off in Rome on the way!" If you thought like that, you were probably coming from somewhere further east. So it was with Paul, whose adventures to spread the gospel had taken him up through Syria to Turkey and across to Greece. He wrote his letter to the Romans while in Corinth. His trip to Spain was not for tourism but to continue his reach westwards across the world of his time.

## Risking Going to Rome?

Paul's mission was to take the gospel to the gentiles, fulfilling his deep conviction that God had appointed him envoy or apostle to the gentiles. He has been busy, as he explains:

> This is the reason that I have so often been hindered from coming to you. But now, with no further place for me in these regions, I desire, as I have for many years, to come to you when I go to Spain. For I do hope to see you on my journey and to be sent on by you, once I have enjoyed your company for a little while. At present, however, I am going to Jerusalem in a ministry to the saints. (Rom 15:22–24)

There was some urgency because, he believed, time was short: Jesus would soon return. Prophecy would soon come true. Before he embarked on his journey, he had another task that belonged to his personal role in these events of the last days. It had been asked of him by James, Peter, and John, when he met with them in Jerusalem, as he explains in Galatians: "When James and Cephas and John, who were acknowledged pillars, recognized the grace that had been given to me, they gave to Barnabas and me the right hand of fellowship, agreeing that we should go to the Gentiles and they to the circumcised. They asked only one thing, that we remember the poor, which was actually what I was eager to do" (Gal 2:9–10).

Therefore, he goes on to explain: "At present, however, I am going to Jerusalem in a ministry to the saints" (Rom 15:25). The prophets had spoken of all the nations flocking to Jerusalem, beating their swords into ploughs and their spears into pruning hooks (Isa 2:2–4) and gathering on Mt Zion for a great feast (Isa 25:6–8). Paul's reinterpretation of this saw not a mass pilgrimage of gentiles to Jerusalem, but a symbolic expression of their solidarity with "the saints," that is, aid for the poor among believers in Jerusalem through generous monetary gifts.

He had previously written to the Corinthians urging that they make such a collection:

> Now concerning the collection for the saints: you should
> follow the directions I gave to the churches of Galatia.
> On the first day of every week, each of you is to put aside
> and save whatever extra you earn, so that collections
> need not be taken when I come. And when I arrive, I will
> send any whom you approve with letters to take your gift
> to Jerusalem. (1 Cor 16:1–3)

In his second letter he reports on the success of this enterprise:

> We want you to know, brothers and sisters, about the grace
> of God that has been granted to the churches of Macedo-
> nia; for during a severe ordeal of affliction, their abundant
> joy and their extreme poverty have overflowed in a wealth
> of generosity on their part. For, as I can testify, they vol-
> untarily gave according to their means, and even beyond

their means, begging us earnestly for the privilege of sharing in this ministry to the saints. (2 Cor 8:1–4)

Part of his reason for reporting this success is that he wants the Corinthians to finish what they had committed themselves to do. He has to be careful not to be too forceful, which might be counterproductive: "I do not say this as a command, but I am testing the genuineness of your love against the earnestness of others" (2 Cor 8:8). He holds before them also the generosity of Jesus:

> For you know the generous act of our Lord Jesus Christ, that though he was rich, yet for your sakes he became poor, so that by his poverty you might become rich. And in this matter I am giving my advice: it is appropriate for you who began last year not only to do something but even to desire to do something—now finish doing it, so that your eagerness may be matched by completing it according to your means. (2 Cor 8:9–11)

Paul exhibits sensitivity, almost careful footwork, in order to press home his concerns:

> Now it is not necessary for me to write to you about the ministry to the saints, for I know your eagerness, which is the subject of my boasting about you to the people of Macedonia, saying that Achaia has been ready since last year; and your zeal has stirred up most of them. But I am sending the brothers in order that our boasting about you may not prove to have been empty in this case, so that you may be ready, as I said you would be; otherwise, if some Macedonians come with me and find that you are not ready, we would be humiliated—to say nothing of you—in this undertaking. So I thought it necessary to urge the brothers to go on ahead to you, and arrange in advance for this bountiful gift that you have promised, so that it may be ready as a voluntary gift and not as an extortion. (2 Cor 9:1–5)

His term for this collection of funds was *koinonia*, the Greek word for fellowship or communion. These new believers would express their solidarity with believers in Judea through their gifts.

In Romans he comes back to the collection because it played
a major role for him. He explains that he will visit them only after
finishing his mission with the collection. Thus, he writes:

> At present, however, I am going to Jerusalem in a min-
> istry to the saints; for Macedonia and Achaia have been
> pleased to share their resources with the poor among the
> saints at Jerusalem. They were pleased to do this, and
> indeed they owe it to them; for if the Gentiles have come
> to share in their spiritual blessings, they ought also to be
> of service to them in material things. So, when I have
> completed this, and have delivered to them what has
> been collected, I will set out by way of you to Spain; and I
> know that when I come to you, I will come in the fullness
> of the blessing of Christ. (Rom 15:25–29)

That visit will be far from straightforward. In a very revealing comment, he continues:

> I appeal to you, brothers and sisters, by our Lord Jesus
> Christ and by the love of the Spirit, to join me in earnest
> prayer to God on my behalf, that I may be rescued from
> the unbelievers in Judea, and that my ministry to Jeru-
> salem may be acceptable to the saints, so that by God's
> will I may come to you with joy and be refreshed in your
> company. The God of peace be with all of you. Amen.
> (Rom 15:30–33)

He was naturally concerned with opposition he might face in Jerusalem from Jews who opposed the movement, but was equally
concerned about a different kind of danger. The followers of Jesus
there in Jerusalem, "the saints," might not find him and his "ministry," namely the collection, acceptable. Why not? Because rumors
had spread that Paul had been teaching that Jews need no longer
live by the Law. Indeed, we see some reflection of this when Luke
recreates the scene of Paul's arrival in Jerusalem and his meeting
with James and the elders. Paul reports on his ministry and Luke
portrays their response:

> When they heard it, they praised God. Then they said
> to him, "You see, brother, how many thousands of

believers there are among the Jews, and they are all zealous for the law. They have been told about you that you teach all the Jews living among the Gentiles to forsake Moses, and that you tell them not to circumcise their children or observe the customs. What then is to be done?" (Acts 21:20–22)

They propose that he use his money to pay for four men among them who had undertaken a ritual vow and who faced the expenditure involved in engaging in the required purification process to render them fit to enter the temple. By doing so, Paul would show that he was completely Law-observant. Luke, writing around three decades later, had indeed portrayed Paul as a hero of the church's expansion and depicted him as always upholding the Law, except where God had set part of it aside, such as the requirement that gentiles joining God's people, gentile converts, be circumcised, the resolution Luke portrays as resolved in the Jerusalem council described in Acts 15.

In reality, the situation was a good deal more complex. For Paul had, indeed, declared that both Jews and gentiles were not bound by Jewish Law and portrayed himself as keeping it when it proved prudent in order not to offend and not keeping it where this was not so. Thus, he writes:

> For though I am free with respect to all, I have made myself a slave to all, so that I might win more of them. To the Jews I became as a Jew, in order to win Jews. To those under the law I became as one under the law (though I myself am not under the law) so that I might win those under the law. To those outside the law I became as one outside the law (though I am not free from God's law but am under Christ's law) so that I might win those outside the law. To the weak I became weak, so that I might win the weak. I have become all things to all people, so that I might by any means save some. I do it all for the sake of the gospel, so that I may share in its blessings. (1 Cor 9:19–23)

Elsewhere, in Galatians, Paul portrays the Law as having fulfilled a role that was now no longer required: "The law was our disciplinarian until Christ came, so that we might be justified by faith. But now that faith has come, we are no longer subject to a disciplinarian, for in Christ Jesus you are all children of God through faith" (Gal 3:25–26). In Romans, he puts it in marital imagery:

> Do you not know, brothers and sisters—for I am speaking to those who know the law—that the law is binding on a person only during that person's lifetime? Thus a married woman is bound by the law to her husband as long as he lives; but if her husband dies, she is discharged from the law concerning the husband. Accordingly, she will be called an adulteress if she lives with another man while her husband is alive. But if her husband dies, she is free from that law, and if she marries another man, she is not an adulteress. In the same way, my friends, you have died to the law through the body of Christ, so that you may belong to another, to him who has been raised from the dead in order that we may bear fruit for God. (Rom 7:1–4)

We cannot really know what happened to Paul's collection in Jerusalem. Did the Jerusalem church, contrary to Luke's account, reject it because they had heard about Paul's attitude towards the Law and so suggest he spend it on helping four men fulfil ritual law? Are there at least some memories of what happened in Luke's account, even though he wrongly portrays Paul as Law observant?

We know from Romans that Paul faced criticism from within the early Jesus movement. Such criticism lies behind his comment in Romans 3 where he refers to what people were saying about his claim that all people are sinners, in that sense, unjust, but that God offers forgiveness and reconciliation:

> But if our injustice serves to confirm the justice of God, what should we say? That God is unjust to inflict wrath on us? (I speak in a human way.) By no means! For then how could God judge the world? But if through my falsehood God's truthfulness abounds to his glory, why am I still being condemned as a sinner? And why not say (as some people slander us by saying that we say), "Let us

do evil so that good may come"? Their condemnation is deserved! (Rom 3:5–8)

He addresses similar slander in Romans 6: "What then are we to say? Should we continue in sin in order that grace may abound? By no means! How can we who died to sin go on living in it?" (Rom 6:1–2). By proclaiming that quite apart from the Law God offered to set us right with himself, Paul did not mean that we are free then to go on to live lawless lives.

Those who believed that all—both Jews and gentiles—should uphold the Law in every aspect that applied to them saw Paul's message as dangerous. They saw him suggesting that people no longer needed the Law. There would be a free for all, they argued. Unfortunately, they had some evidence on their side, for they could point to what had been going on in Corinth. Paul had so many problems to address there, as is evident from his correspondence. That just proved to his opponents that Paul had got it wrong.

People in Rome obviously knew of such allegations against Paul. If, possibly, the Jerusalem church was not willing to make Paul welcome, there would certainly have been some in Rome who would have been reluctant. Paul started the church in Corinth, Ephesus, and elsewhere, but not the church in Rome. Peter had already been there.

"Tread carefully, Paul! You could be in trouble. It could stymie your visit to Spain. Be very careful what you say and how you say it!" Such would probably have been the advice of Paul's friends, and this is precisely what we find when we turn to Paul's letter. He wants to give an account of his gospel, defend it against accusations that he was betraying the faith of Israel, and get the Romans on side. This was much more than wanting to be personally accepted. It was, fundamentally, about his wanting them to share in the richness of the gospel as he understood it. There was a lot at stake.

## Paul Treading Very Carefully

We have seen Paul's sensitivity in seeking to avoid offence else-where in his handling of the collection. It is clearly evident in his opening statements in Romans. Rule number one: find common ground. So, within his opening greeting, he cites a concise state-ment of the gospel with which he knows they will concur:

> Paul, a servant of Jesus Christ, called to be an apostle, set apart for the gospel of God, which he promised before-hand through his prophets in the holy scriptures, the gos-pel concerning his Son, who was descended from David according to the flesh and was declared to be Son of God with power according to the spirit of holiness by resurrec-tion from the dead, Jesus Christ our Lord. (Rom 1:1-4)

He is at the same time claiming his authority as "a servant of Jesus Christ" and an "apostle." He goes on to spell out the latter in terms that were probably familiar, assuming they were aware of Paul's role as agreed by James, Cephas (Peter), and John, cited above. Accordingly, Paul goes on to say in his opening statement to the Romans: "through whom we have received grace and apostleship to bring about the obedience of faith among all the Gentiles for the sake of his name, including yourselves who are called to belong to Jesus Christ" (Rom 1:5-6). This goes beyond reminding them of his status. It also indicates that he intends to engage in ministry among them. How would they receive that?

Immediately, having completed his greeting, Paul deals with any potential hesitancy by praising them: "First, I thank my God through Jesus Christ for all of you, because your faith is proclaimed throughout the world" (Rom 1:8). More than that, he assures them: "For God, whom I serve with my spirit by announcing the gospel of his Son, is my witness that without ceasing I remember you always in my prayers, asking that by God's will I may somehow at last succeed in coming to you" (Rom 1:9-10). He wants them to know his genuine concern for them. This is very positive.

He continues: "For I am longing to see you so that I may share with you some spiritual gift to strengthen you" (Rom 1:11).

Careful, Paul, at this point! He is careful and takes a step back, immediately adding: "or rather so that we may be mutually encouraged by each other's faith, both yours and mine" (Rom 1:12). He needed to balance his sense of his own authority and gifts with the acknowledgement that they, too, might have something to offer.

He comes back to his intent: "I want you to know, brothers and sisters, that I have often intended to come to you (but thus far have been prevented), in order that I may reap some harvest among you as I have among the rest of the Gentiles" (Rom 1:13). Had there been some criticism about his not having come before this? As we have seen, he comes back to the issues in Romans 15, where again he explains why he had not yet been there. He had been too busy in his mission elsewhere: "This is the reason that I have so often been hindered from coming to you. But now, with no further place for me in these regions, I desire, as I have for many years, to come to you when I go to Spain" (Rom 15:22–23).

Paul's sensitivity continues as he explains why he intends to visit: "I am a debtor both to Greeks and to barbarians, both to the wise and to the foolish—hence my eagerness to proclaim the gospel to you also who are in Rome" (Rom 1:14–15). As he had introduced himself as the servant/slave of Christ in 1:1, here he adopts the lowly pose of a debtor. Paul is seeking to make clear that he has no interest in a takeover of Rome's house churches or in enjoying the exercise of power, as preachers and leaders can. Fear not! I simply want to share with you in the gospel. It matters! A debtor is a humble image.

## Now to the Point

This brings Paul to one of the major matters he needs to address: his controversial gospel: "For I am not ashamed of the gospel; it is the power of God for salvation to everyone who has faith, to the Jew first and also to the Greek" (Rom 1:16). Paul's words have been the subject of controversy far beyond his own day and need a little explanation. He is speaking about "salvation," meaning not simply surviving judgement day, but doing so because one has been acquitted and is in a positive relationship with God.

The focus on "everyone" relates to the way Paul has become known for saying that all people obtain salvation the same way. "Jew" and "Greek" means *everyone*. He uses "Greek" as a term for everyone not a Jew. "Who has faith" identifies the key to Paul's argument about how they obtain salvation: by believing and receiving what is offered. "The Jew first" acknowledges that the gospel came first to Jews through Jesus.

He sees no reason to back down from the gospel he preaches, despite the pressure from some. He is about to expound why and so opens with a statement bolstered with biblical support: "For in it the righteousness of God is revealed through faith for faith; as it is written, 'The one who is righteous will live by faith'" (Rom 1:17). This statement, too, has been subject to controversy. "The righteousness of God" is not an abstract statement about how good God is, as if to say the gospel wants people to know that God is good, not bad. The meaning is stronger than that: God's goodness is God's generosity. Jewish tradition could speak of God's goodness and say that this was why God was willing to help people, even forgive them and restore them.

In the gospel, God's goodness and generosity is open for all to see, it is "revealed." Paul again uses the word "faith." This is how God's goodness and generosity is appropriated: faith sees it and faith believes it, that is, "through faith for faith." Paul quotes Haggai to support his point: "The one who is righteous will live by faith." "The one who is righteous" means the person who has been set in a right relationship with God because of God's generosity and goodness. "Will live" does not so much mean how they will behave in everyday life, but something more like: "will have eternal life," in that sense, will have the salvation promised in the gospel. How? By believing the offer of a restored relationship with God and embracing it. Paul wants to emphasize that this is the same basis for everyone.

## Launching His Defense

He is now about to launch into the defense of his gospel. It will run until the end of chapter 3 where we find the same words coming back again. "But now, irrespective of [or apart from] law, the righteousness of God has been disclosed, and is attested by the law and the prophets, the righteousness of God through faith in Jesus Christ for all who believe" (Rom 3:21–22). God's goodness offering restoration of a right relationship with God has been made possible because God offered it through Jesus and it is to be embraced as a gift by faith, by believing and taking it on board.

In between Paul mounts his argument. A key element is the argument that *everyone is in the same boat,* whether a Jew or a gentile. As he goes on in the summary to state: "all have sinned and fall short of the glory of God" (Rom 3:23). Earlier, he addressed the issue of whether Jews were somehow not to be counted or were exempt, speaking of himself as a Jew: "What then? Are we any better off? No, not at all; for we have already charged that all, both Jews and Greeks, are under the power of sin" (Rom 3:9). He goes on to bolster this claim with a string of biblical quotations affirming that all are sinners (Rom 3:10–18) and concludes by underlining that fact that these had to include Jews because they were addressed to them: "Now we know that whatever the law says, it speaks to those who are under the law, so that every mouth may be silenced, and the whole world may be held accountable to God. For 'no human being will be justified in his sight' by deeds prescribed by the law, for through the law comes the knowledge of sin" (Rom 3:19–20).

## Starting on Common Ground: Sexual Perversion and Depravity

He reached this point in his argument by first starting with common ground. Those listening to his letter in Roman house churches would have included Jews like himself as well as former converts to Judaism, commonly called proselytes, and gentiles won to the faith. Former converts to Judaism are likely to have been particularly sensitive to anyone seeming to undermine their new faith, so Paul must tread carefully.

He obviously decided to start with something on which all would have agreed: the depravity of the outside world. The Book of Wisdom had linked perverted approaches to God in the form of idolatry to perverted human behavior. In 1 Thessalonians Paul had linked not knowing God to sexual wrongdoing and in 1 Corinthians 10 had done the same, as we saw at the conclusion of the last chapter. Here he follows the same path. Thus, he begins his argument with a clear statement about God's anger against such depravity. "For the wrath of God is revealed from heaven against all ungodliness and wickedness of those who by their wickedness suppress the truth" (Rom 1:18). At the core of such depravity is people's failure to acknowledge God as God. As he goes on to point out, people should have recognized God through observing creation and so are without excuse.

Not only did they not recognize God as God, but "they became futile in their thinking, and their senseless minds were darkened. Claiming to be wise, they became fools; and they exchanged the glory of the immortal God for images resembling a mortal human being or birds or four-footed animals or reptiles" (Rom 1:21–22). Their failure to recognize God resulted in a serious psychological flaw that had them foolishly imagining images of humans and animals as gods. This was an exchange, a perversion of reality.

It had further consequences, argued Paul, to which God abandoned them: "Therefore God gave them up in the lusts of their hearts to impurity, to the degrading of their bodies among themselves, because they exchanged the truth about God for a lie and worshipped and served the creature rather than the Creator, who is blessed for ever! Amen" (Rom 1:24–25). Not only did their mind create a perverted image of God—*they themselves* became perverted. "The lusts of their hearts" means the passions generated in their minds. As the context goes on to show, these are sexual passions. Sexual passions are never evil in Paul, but when they take control of a person they lead people into "impurity." "Impurity" here is not referring to ritual impurity. Ritual impurity was just a part of everyday life, like being ritually impure during menstruation, after intercourse, or after childbirth—all perfectly healthy aspects of living. The "impurity" Paul writes about here is moral impurity, and sexual immorality in particular, as he used also in 1 Thessalonians (4:7).

"The degrading of their bodies among themselves" needs some explanation and that will follow. Clearly it refers to something happening between people. "Degrading" means that something degrades, dishonors, and treats their bodies in a way that brings shame on them. The following context will explain why these actions brought about shame and meant that these people by these actions should be ashamed.

First, however, Paul reinforces his claim that such behavior is the result of distortion. The word "exchanged" occurs again in 1:25 as it had in 1:23. It is a key word. Something goes on that changes things from what they ought to be. Having a perverted understanding of God produces a perverted mind and perverted behavior.

In 1:26 Paul repeats the consequences of perverse understandings of God: God gives people up to be ruled by their sexual passions. "Their women exchanged natural intercourse for unnatural" (1:26). Literally, the Greek refers to "females." "Their" is from a male perspective, thinking of women as belonging to or with men. We have the word "exchange" again, indicating that they are changing something from what it ought to be. What are they changing? Paul writes of "natural intercourse." As a Jew of his time, and like most people of his time, he would understand "natural intercourse" as vaginal intercourse between a man and a woman.

What then would Paul mean by "unnatural" intercourse? Paul does not tell us. People have canvassed a range of options: anal intercourse with a man, which was a common form of contraceptive, oral sex, sex with animals, sex with other women. Any of these options might fit, but in the light of what follows the more likely behavior being addressed is sex between women, not least because, as we have seen, in extant Jewish literature of the time male-male and female-female sexual relations are sometimes linked. Paul's transition, "in the same way," as he continues, may also indicate this. For Paul goes on speak of men and here same-gender sex is clearly in view:

> . . . and in the same way also the men, giving up natural intercourse with women, were consumed with passion for one another. Men committed shameless acts with men and received in their own persons the due penalty for their error. (Rom 1:27)

Again, the text speaks literally of "males." Paul writes of "natural intercourse with females," making it likely that we should read the statement about females and "natural intercourse" as meaning "natural intercourse with males." With the males it is clear. They are "consumed with [literally: burning with] passion for one another." This coheres with what Paul had said earlier, namely that God abandoned people to be ruled by their sexual passions. "For one another" suggests that Paul has consenting sex between men in mind.

"Shameless acts" recalls Paul's word in 1:24 about degrading bodies. Here he is speaking of acts of which men should be ashamed, because one man assumed a woman's role and the other had him do so. More significant still was the shame of acting contrary to what God made you to be. What Paul meant by males receiving "in their own persons the due penalty for their error" (Rom 1:27) is unclear. It may refer to soreness of the penis or of the anus or perhaps some other discomfort.

In the words that follow, Paul returns to where he began, the basis of his analysis: "And since they did not see fit to acknowledge God, God gave them up to a debased [literally: an unfit] mind and to things that should not be done" (Rom 1:28). With its word play on "fit," obscured in many translations, it summarizes Paul's argument: an unfit acknowledgement of God resulted in an unfit mind and unfitting actions. Perversion produces perversion. It is a psychological argument.

From these words, Paul goes beyond the issues of same-gender sexual relations to list a range of other sins that result from the sinful state of mind, concluding: "They know God's decree, that those who practice such things deserve to die—yet they not only do them but even applaud others who practice them" (Rom 1:32). This may hark back in part to the theme of homosexual relations, especially in the allusion to the death penalty, which does not apply for most of the sins listed, but does for what Leviticus condemns—men sleeping with men: "If a man lies with a male as with a woman, both of them have committed an abomination; they shall be put to death; their blood is upon them" (Lev 20:15). The reference to people applauding such sinful practices (Rom 1:32) may also allude to same-gender sexual relations and their toleration and approval in some circles.

By the time those listening to Paul's letter being read aloud had reached this point in his argument, we can imagine many nods of approval. What he was saying was very similar to what had been said in the Book of Wisdom about idolatry having consequences in human behavior. Paul would probably have had his hearers well onside. It was standard proclamation. There was nothing controversial about it. It was what all such hearers would have assumed.

It has been suggested that some may have thought, in particular, about the goings on in imperial circles of earlier days, with Gaius Caligula or Nero. Others may have known, as has been suggested, of predatory Stoic teachers exploiting their students. For most, Paul was simply pointing to well known facts and highlighting the perversions of his time. "Good on-ya, Paul!" might have been their response.

## Paul's Rhetorical Twist

The person reading the letter out loud then continued and the atmosphere will have changed. Suddenly they hear Paul's words: "Therefore you have no excuse, whoever you are, when you judge others; for in passing judgement on another you condemn yourself, because you, the judge, are doing the very same things" (Rom 2:1). Paul was an educated man and that meant he had learned how to compose speeches to good effect. Softening people up and then landing a solid blow was great rhetorical technique. He was not being abusive because what he had written made sense. Of course, if you do the same things, you are worthy of just as much condemnation as anyone else.

Paul was not suggesting that his hearers were engaged in the same-gender sexual behavior he had just condemned, but they were, nevertheless, involved in sin. He even takes his sensitive concession about "the Jew first" and turns it around: "There will be anguish and distress for everyone who does evil, the Jew first and also the Greek, but glory and honor and peace for everyone who does good, the Jew first and also the Greek. For God shows no partiality" (Rom 2:9–10). This was the point of the exercise: to show his fellow Jews that they, too, were sinners, just like the wicked gentile world, and so they, too, needed what Paul offered in his gospel. Having the Law was, of course, an advantage for Jews, but counted for nothing if they broke the Law. All have sinned. All need God's forgiveness. So, all need the gospel Paul preached and he was in no way going to retreat from it.

## Understanding Paul on Same-Gender Sexual Relations

The setting for Paul's few comments about same-gender sexual relations is within an argument designed to defend his gospel. He could have chosen other examples of sin in the wider world, but this was in some sense a favorite because it was widely perceived at the time as so blatantly wrong. Both he and his audience will have seen it as such.

Paul will have shared, with those who were to listen to his letter, the view that God made humankind male and female. His use of "males" and "females" may well be echoing this text. This was the standard assumption shared, we noted in our earlier chapter, with fellow Jewish authors whose works have survived. All human beings are heterosexual. When someone who is by nature created male has desire towards another male, a distortion has taken place in his being. Paul connects this distortion or perversion to distortion and perversion in people's understanding of God. That is where it comes from. Something goes wrong with their minds.

Paul argues psychologically. He writes of people becoming "futile in their thinking," having "senseless minds" that were "darkened" (1:21) and having "unfit minds" (1:28).

It made sense to Paul, on the basis of his presuppositions about all people being created naturally heterosexual, to understand gay and lesbian orientations as a distortion, a perversion of the mind resulting from sin. He does not relate it to Adam's sin, as though it had been a consequence of the fall that some people are born this way. For him, they are not born that way. It is, rather, the outcome of not acknowledging God. Get it wrong about God and everything goes wrong. That was a standard argument. In such perverted minds, he argued, people chose to let passions rule. The healthy mind rules the passions, our God-given desires, but in these minds, according to Paul, passions have become misdirected and strong and these people surrender to them. Others, too, attributed such misdirection to the strength of one's passions. For Paul, therefore, the sin was not just the act, as though everything is fine as long as you are celibate and don't act on your feelings. Nor was the sin only when you harbored the desire to act, whether you did or not. Sin was your state of being corrupted and perverted by sin, as a result of which you have the desire and might act on it.

Such desire and behavior was unnatural, according to Paul, not because of some theory about biological parts fitting together, the penis and vagina. If at all, such thoughts would have been seen as part of a more important broader view of nature—an understanding of how God created a person. To act contrary to your nature as God created you, and to have such feelings and such orientation, was to be and act contrary to God and God's will.

Paul was not limiting his attention just to acts. Nor was he limiting his attention to particular settings, as though he was concerned only when such behavior took place in idolatrous settings. That misses the point that his argument was not primarily about actions but about persons and their perverted state, which produced the perverted behavior. Paul may well have included a broad sweep of such abuses in his condemnation—including pedophilia, abuse of slaves, male rape, but he was clearly also writing about non-exploitive relations, mutual consensual sex between people of the same-gender.

His concern with passions was not just about their strength. Clearly, their power was a part of it, for he sees letting them dominate as one of the characteristics leading to same-gender sexual acts. For Paul, however, it was more than that. It was having what he would understand as an unnaturally directed or oriented passion in the first place.

Some have suggested that Paul was merely writing about heterosexual men and women who engage in same-gender sexual acts, and that he makes no comment on gay men, lesbians, and bisexuals (who do not fall foul of his argument, it is argued, because they are only behaving in ways that are natural to them). The problem with this argument is that nothing indicates that Paul believed there were such people. He almost certainly would have agreed with Philo in rejecting claims that some people were naturally gay. For Paul, everyone was heterosexual and if your mind, feelings, or actions run contrary to this, then you are in a serious state of sin. For that, Paul believes there is restoration and redemption, including bringing you back to be normal, as God meant you to be.

It is sometimes difficult to stand back and appreciate the nature of Paul's argument. His approach generally, which gave attention to people's state of being, and not just to their actions, was profound. In Romans and elsewhere, he argues that the problem for humanity is primarily not sins but sin, *a state of being*. In his view, change comes about for people when they get their relationship with God right. It is not something they can achieve on their own. It is a gift of God's generosity. Accept that generosity, that offer of a restored relationship with God, and things will begin to change. The Spirit, the manifestation of God's love, will not only assure you of forgiveness but will deal with your fear, releasing you to be a bearer of God's Spirit and life in the world. Your life will then bear the fruit of the Spirit, which Paul lists as "love, joy, peace, patience, kindness, generosity, faithfulness, gentleness, and self-control" (Gal 5:22–23). Such love, greater than faith and hope, is the primary mark of the Spirit and shows itself in attitudes and acts of love. These more than fulfil what the Law was meant to achieve. God's goodness and generosity thus generates goodness and generosity in us.

Paul applies these insights to what he sees has gone wrong when people engage in what he sees as being perverted sexual acts, reflecting perverted desires, and a perverted state of sin of the self. His assessment should not be dismissed as in every case inappropriate. For some, he might be spot-on and lead to the possibility of healing and renewal. Who can know? But in a world where, increasingly, people are realizing that the assumption that all people are heterosexual by nature needs updating and is, indeed, incorrect, we have to treat Paul's few verses—told to illustrate the world's depravity—with great care.

It is, to my mind, an abuse to impose on Paul, on dogmatic grounds, a requirement that he must have had a comprehensive understanding of human sexuality. Such abuse employs all kinds of intellectual gymnastics to try to harmonize Paul with what we now know. Let Paul be Paul and love him. Why can we not allow Paul to be a person who did not know everything about human sexuality? That means allowing that he was a man of his world who has given us so much, but from within a worldview determined by the assumptions of his time.

What do we do with this material? That will be the focus of our next chapter.

# 8

# Where Do We Go from Here?

"You're the ones who are obsessed with sex, not me! If you think your uncle and I have been obsessed with sex over these last thirty years, you've got it all wrong. Would you say that of your mum and dad? Marriage and partnership is about much more than sex. Give us a break!"

Helen recoiled. Uncle Andrew was clearly angry, but also a little sad. She could see it in his eyes. He had always been her favorite. He was kind and gentle. He would listen to her. With him she always felt safe. She could talk to him, so this set her back somewhat.

She explained. "You see, I've been reading this book, *Sex, Then and Now*, and it tells how the people who wrote the Bible, like Paul, saw same-gender sexual relations as sin, really bad sin. It was all because the brains of people doing such things had been messed up, starting with not acknowledging God and so they were messed up in their feelings and their actions. Men fell in love with men instead of with women and women did the same."

Her uncle sat back in his chair. "Of course, they thought like that and many still do. In some countries it is still in their legislation. Sodomy, as they put it, is a criminal offence. It was on our books, too, until last century. People saw gay people as depraved perverts."

Helen was very aware that her uncle was well informed. He had made a significant contribution to the community through his work in the legal profession and was very highly regarded.

"You need to understand," her uncle went on to explain, "that people assumed that if you were attracted to those of your own sex you were somehow sick or evil. Sometimes the church spread that view by repeating the judgements expressed in the Bible, but sometimes it wasn't religious at all. Men often saw themselves as needing to be strong and manly, and so many men felt very uncomfortable with contemplating men loving other men, let alone seeing them give expression to it. They squirmed."

Helen could understand that. "But it wasn't like that with women," she said. "It seemed quite okay for women to live together and be close friends and partners. I suppose it's different with women."

"Yes," her uncle replied. "No one bothered much about women. In fact, until only recently, no one bothered much about men having close friendships, either. It was all very normal and natural and then the gay issues came along, and you can't be close friends with another man now without people asking or thinking: Are they gay? Do they have sex? The word 'gay' used to simply mean, 'happy'. Now, for some it's a death sentence."

"That's very sad," reflected Helen. "It must be hard."

"There were always some men who got into sex with other men in wild parties, usually the types who would sleep around with women and with men," added her uncle. "There were male prostitutes and there still are. Some flout it—in your face! So, yes, Paul was right. Some were like that and that's probably all he knew. But there are others who are not at all like that. It's just the way they are."

Helen nodded. Her uncle was one of them. She felt a little ashamed to have implied that because he and his partner had been together for years, they must somehow be obsessed with sex. Come to think of it, that was absurd and so insulting. And he was right:

she wouldn't say that about her parents or other married people. Marriage is about much more than sex. To think otherwise is really a perversion.

While she was still a little sunken in regret, her uncle continued: "You see, with women, they're not like men. They don't relate sexually in the same way. So people imagined they didn't have real sex or experience sexual highs like men. But this is, of course, nonsense. Sex is not just about men and about male penetration. Sex is also about much more than experiencing orgasm. Sexual attraction and fulfilment may be present across a whole range of behaviors, from holding hands, a gentle embrace, or a kiss, to more ecstatic forms."

This was getting a little personal and explicit. Helen knew what he meant. "And sometimes hugging has nothing to do with sex," she added.

"Yes," replied her uncle. "We must get away from this obsessive idea that everything in a relationship of friendship is about sex or that sex is present only when someone has an orgasm. That's a distortion."

Helen was not about to ask her uncle about private aspects of his partnership, but it had never occurred to her that it was all about sex with them. It obviously wasn't. How hard it must be, she thought, to be gay. You'd have people always seeing you through a sexual lens. Awful! She simply summed up her reflections, saying: "It must be hard to be gay."

Helen sensed from Andrew's eyes that this had touched a nerve, but he didn't respond. Instead, he explained: "You see, there are lots of misconceptions. You can have close personal friendships and partnerships with people of your own gender without sex playing a role or playing a major role. We must stop imagining that sex equals sexual intercourse. There is so much more to sex. We must also stop assuming that people are either gay or straight. Some people are very gay. Some people are very straight. Some people are a little of both. And what's more, it doesn't always remain the same. There are women who were happily married who in later life form lesbian relationships. It just happens that way."

That set Helen wondering about her friends. That's what some meant when they said they were non-binary. She had also heard about people undergoing so-called "conversion therapy," now illegal in many states. Even many gay people who are committed to celibacy, some of whom had gone to such therapy, declare it unacceptable and damaging.

Andrew continued: "People can change over the years. It is not uncommon for people going through adolescence to have a range of sexual feelings. They may go straight through it—pardon the pun—but they may have a phase when they are oriented differently from usual. The important thing is: don't force people to define themselves. Keep open. Things do sometimes change for people, and that can happen at any stage of life."

Helen reflected on her own experience, but that was private. Had she ever felt feelings for another girl? And what about her friend who is clearly attracted mainly to other girls? Did that friend sometimes have feelings for boys?

While Helen was pondering these possibilities, Andrew began again and this time you could see in his eyes that it was personal. "You see, I can remember a time at school. The other kids saw me with this guy. I was really fond of him. We did lots of things together, but nothing serious. The other kids saw us holding hands once and that started it. We got called 'poofters,' 'faggots.' 'perverts.' The names were bearable, but one afternoon after school they cornered my friend and beat him up."

Tears came into Andrew's eyes. "Yes, that happened. I was lucky. He didn't report what had happened because he was scared of what the teachers would think. I know of other men for whom it was much, much worse. Some committed suicide. Girls, too. History is littered with persecution of gay and lesbian people. Yes, and sometimes it was the church that inspired the hate. There are still gay hate crimes. Your pastor should be preaching against that instead of preaching against gays."

Helen's uncle didn't go to church. Perhaps this was why. Sensitive as usual, he realized that attacking Helen's pastor might have been going a little too far, but it was true. So, he suggested the name of a minister of another local church, where he knew there was a commitment to openness and gay folk felt welcome. Helen appreciated that.

The conversation came to end. It had been so helpful. It had set Helen thinking in new ways and with deep feeling. In some ways she felt quite upset and that afternoon took herself off for a walk in the local woods. There was her favorite rock where she loved to sit, looking at the trees and listening to the birds. It was a place to be close to God.

This time she was listening to herself, her feelings, her thoughts. She prayed. "O God, I'm sorry. I'm so sad. I'm sorry I thought about gay people like that. I'm so sorry." And, yes, it made her cry. What else could she say? What else could she pray? "O God, help me, forgive me. Help me to show kindness and care for people suffering because of their sexuality, because of what others do to them and because of what they do to themselves. Help me to help and spread understanding. Your words are about freedom and health and wholeness. And thank you for Uncle Andrew."

Her prayer ended but said so much more than her words. It was like her whole body prayed, and, as it did, her whole body and mind found rest and peace. But a lot more was happening. She felt a renewed energy welling up inside her. She was going to stand up for love. She was going to stand up for justice.

That evening she saw Uncle Andrew again and told him what had happened. He listened. It was moving for him, too. He looked her in the eye with love and affection and said:

"Never let go of love. Never let go of truth. Never let go of hope. Never let go of understanding and openness. Some people will not see it your way. Love and respect them, too. Some gay people resolve to remain celibate. Yes, they have close friendships, but they set limits on what they do. They see that as upholding biblical commands. They don't have it easy. Love and respect them. They're on the journey, too."

Helen had heard about people like that. Surely, it's okay for them to do that—as long as they don't try to impose it on others. She also knew of others who claimed to be Bible believers and who used Scripture to condemn even those celibate gay people. They needed to be challenged because, despite claiming to do so, they were not taking the Bible seriously. These days we have learned the importance of hearing people from other cultures in the light of their culture and that cannot be any different from hearing the biblical writers. Respect doesn't mean you have to adopt everything another culture believes.

Helen was in her first year of a university degree and had already enjoyed being exposed to people with different points of view. There really are people who believe the world is flat, that God made it just six thousand years ago and hid fossils in the ground to make it seem older. There really are people who account for mental illnesses by speaking of demon possession. And there really are people who believe that human beings are all heterosexual and that being gay is not real, but a sinful perversion.

Helen was clear that to love other people did not necessarily mean agreeing with them. Argument and conflict can happen with respect. It is good to challenge ideas. That's how you learn.

For all of that, what Helen found most convincing was not the arguments, but the *people*. In particular, her Uncle Andrew was the best evidence. Now that it is becoming more acceptable for people who are genuinely gay to identify themselves as such, this living evidence abounds. The media has made it mainstream. There are simply too many people like Uncle Andrew for Helen or any of us to hold onto the old prejudices. Prejudices? Yes—prejudging people's relationships as necessarily perverse and sinful because one is treating Paul's observations as comprehensively accurate of all such friendships.

Helen had been waiting to ask about her brother: "Uncle Andrew, do you think my brother Kevin might have inherited a gay gene in the family?"

Andrew, who was well acquainted with research, replied: "No, I don't think it works that way. At least, so far, no one has identified a so-called gay gene. Nothing is inevitable. But you've been a great sister to him. That will have been so important and will continue to be in the future."

Helen smiled. Yes, it was true. She replied: "Thanks, Uncle Andrew, that's my hope and prayer."

Indeed, it was. Her faith, now better informed, meant even more effective love and hope, not just for Kevin but also for all LGBTQI people who would cross her path.

We are invited to join her.

# Afterword

WHILE PREPARING THIS BOOK, I received an inquiry about these issues from someone deeply conflicted. I share my response:

Dear———,

Thank you for your email.

I understand what it means to come from an evangelical/fundamentalist background, because those were also my beginnings, which I still value in many ways. I grasped then that I could trust God and need never be afraid to ask questions and explore.

I have never given up my evangelical conviction that the most important thing in life is to have a restored relationship with God. It was in fact my faith that led me to study, ministry, and research, and in doing so to take the Bible seriously, more seriously than I had when I was a fundamentalist, when I saw it as a timeless infallible book.

Taking the Bible seriously for me meant reading it carefully, learning Greek and Hebrew so that I could pick up its fine points, and deepening my understanding of its religious and cultural context.

So I embarked on a journey that many have taken and which began internationally in the eighteenth century, beginning with the realization that the Bible is not a single-authored book. It is two collections, one in Hebrew, one in Greek, and more than that, the New Testament was a collection of works by individual authors, each with their own style.

With the Gospels, in particular, it was very clear that there were four versions of the same basic story, but also that the first three were often identical to the point that they must have been connected in some way, leading to the widespread conclusion that Mark was written first and that Matthew and Luke independently supplemented Mark. I remember exploring their three versions of the one story and noticing both how well they fitted together and also where there were clear difference in style and content. Most dramatically this was apparent in the differences between the first three and John. John has Jesus' ministry last three years and has him die when the lambs were slain the afternoon before Passover Day, whereas the first three have Jesus' ministry last just one year and have him die on Passover Day.

Taking the Bible seriously meant, for me, realizing that these authors were people bearing witness to their faith in their way, making use of their information Through their witness to God's Word and action they had become vehicles through which God spoke and speaks to us. Their words are *their* words, *not* the words of God nor words somehow supernaturally dictated or controlled by God.

The differences I mention above (and there are, of course, plenty more) would make that an impossible idea. The statement of faith of the church to which I belong, the Uniting Church in Australia (formed when Methodists, Presbyterians, and Congregational churches united in 1977) declares that the Scriptures are witnesses to the Word, and the Word is Jesus.

Cross-cultural encounter with respect has to be central to our approach to these writings, as I see it. I must always be on my guard not to hear only what I want to hear or read into their words what I want to find. It is also the rule for any personal encounter with others.

I, therefore, respect that they will have believed that the universe came into being just six thousand years ago, that the earth was flat (or if they knew some Greek philosophy, that the world was round and the sun circled it), that human reproduction happened when the male placed the seed/the fertilized egg in the female womb, that, generally, men were superior to women, that arid soil and prickly plants came about because of Adam's sin, and much more.

Of course, they were people of their time. We would have believed the same had we lived then. It is not for us to feel superior because we know that none of those beliefs turned out to be correct. We may have more knowledge but that does not mean we are wiser. Their witness was human AND God speaks through their witness, despite their speaking a different language and reflecting different assumptions from us on many things.

Where do same-gender sexual relations fit into this? Some people in their world did believe that some people were born gay and some, the vast majority, were born straight. All our evidence indicates that Jews, and that includes those who formed the Christian movement, rejected such beliefs.

They took Gen 1:27 (God made male and female) seriously as their science and so concluded that all people were by nature heterosexual and that people having an orientation, and feelings, let alone acting on them towards members of their own gender, were acting contrary to their nature and to how God made them. They took the prohibitions of Leviticus 18 and 20 and applied them more widely to condemn all such same-sex behavior.

Given what their science told them, that all makes sense. Paul can therefore use such same-gender orientation and behavior in Romans 1 as his illustration of the wider world's depravity because he knew the believers in Rome would agree with him. It was uncontroversial. His list in 1 Corinthians 6:9–10 very probably refers to active and passive gays, as does 1 Timothy 1:10 to the active partner. This is how Jews of the time understood it and it must have also seemed very reasonable, especially when you looked at male and female bodies. It was obvious how they should fit together.

It has taken a long time for us to realize that the matter is not so simple. Some people are not born male or female but have mixed genitalia. Inside, some people also have mixed sexual orientation and some are primarily attracted to people of their own gender. They are a small but not insignificant minority.

I remember once when I was running a workshop in a farming area and farmers saying, "Of course!" This is also the case among our cattle. In fact, we now realize that this is something that occurs in the animal world. We, too, are mammals.

Does it show disrespect to Paul or to the Bible to suggest he and its authors did not know everything there is to know about sex? Of course, not. True hallowing of Scripture means taking it seriously in its own terms and its own world and engaging with it. The world is not flat. People are not all heterosexual.

This means that it would be irresponsible to take what Paul says based on his assumptions and apply it in contexts where we know that his assumptions need updating. Yes, there will be some who are just as Paul put it, heterosexuals who have messed up their sexuality, but there are others for whom this is not so.

Now that it has become safe for people and the media to talk openly about same-gender sexual relations, we have come to recognize many wonderful people, leaders in the community, in churches, in government, in the arts, and generally, who are highly regarded human beings. The existence of such real people, even better, meeting them, can be so much more persuasive than arguments.

There are two key aspects that, I have observed, play a role in the struggle many people have. First: how to understand the Bible. The first Christian believers had to face this question when they ventured with their mission out into the non-Jewish world. Scripture was clear: non-Jews joining the people of God must be circumcised (Genesis 17) and there were other parts of the biblical Law that also applied to them, and Jews should keep the whole Law.

They compromised, setting circumcision and many other requirements aside. There was outrage from the fundamentalists.

They sought to undo Paul's mission in Galatia provoking his terse response. Paul had found himself earlier in conflict with fellow Jewish believers persuaded by people from James in Jerusalem to keep strictly to the biblical Law as they saw it and not eat regularly with non-Jews. He reports it in Galatians 2:11–14. His partner Barnabas abandoned him along with Peter.

Paul's argument was that God's grace overrode such laws. In other words, generally, they read and applied Scripture not on the basis of its letter but its *spirit*, its *heart*, and, where need be, set aside such requirements. Mark interprets Jesus as doing so in Mark 7 in declaring all foods clean, for instance.

The second aspect is: what do we now know to be the truth about sexuality? Is everyone heterosexual, as Paul and his fellow Jews believed, or not? In other words, do we, like Paul reconsidering circumcision and similar laws, face a situation not envisaged by the Bible's writers, including Paul, himself? Most, with good reason, would say: Yes, we do. Then we embrace people and their sexualities with love and acceptance and with the encouragement that in all things love rules, as for straight people, so for all.

I hope this proves useful.


Bill Loader

# For Further Reading

My detailed discussions of matters of sexualities are to be found in the following publications.

## On same-sex sexual relations specifically:

"Homosexuality in the New Testament." SBL *Odyssey* (2018): http://bibleodyssey.org/en/passages/related-articles/homosexuality-in-the-new-testament/.

"Homosexuality: Judaism Second Temple and Hellenistic Judaism." In *Encyclopaedia of the Bible and Its Reception* 12, edited by Constance M. Furey et al., 301–3. Berlin: de Gruyter, 2016.

"Paul on Same-Sex Relations in Romans 1." *Interpretation* 74.2 (2020) 242–52. https://doi.org/10.1177/0020964320921962. Also in William R. G. Loader, *Jesus Left Loose Ends: Collected Essays*, 265–79. Adelaide: Australian Theological Forum, 2021.

"Reading Romans 1 on Homosexuality in the Light of Biblical/Jewish and Greco-Roman Perspectives of Its Time." *Zeitschrift für die neutestamentliche Wissenschaft* 108 (2017) 119–49. Also in William R. G. Loader, *Sexuality and Gender. Collected Essays*, 349–78. WUNT 458. Tübingen: Mohr Siebeck, 2021.

"Same-Sex Relationships: A 1st-Century Perspective." *Harvard Theological Studies* 70.1 (2014) 423–31. doi: 10.4102/hts.v70i1.2114. http://www.hts.org.za/index.php/HTS/article/view/2114/.

## On passages/related-articles/
## homosexuality-in-the-new-testament

with Megan K. DeFranza, Wesley Hill, and Stephen R. Holmes, *Two Views on Homosexuality, the Bible, and the Church*. Counterpoints: Bible and Theology, edited by Preston Sprinkle. Grand Rapids: Zondervan, 2016. (Korean translation: Seoul: Korean IVP, 2018.)

## On same-sex sexual relations
## alongside sexuality generally:

I have written five major research volumes in attitudes towards sexuality in the broadest sense in early Jewish and Christian literature to the end of the first century CE.

*Enoch, Levi, and Jubilees on Sexuality: Attitudes Towards Sexuality in the Early Enoch Literature, the Aramaic Levi Document, and the Book of Jubilees.* Grand Rapids: Eerdmans, 2007.

*The Dead Sea Scrolls on Sexuality: Attitudes Towards Sexuality in Sectarian and Related Literature at Qumran.* Grand Rapids: Eerdmans, 2009.

*The Pseudepigrapha on Sexuality: Attitudes Towards Sexuality in Apocalypses, Testament, Legends, Wisdom, and Related Literature.* Grand Rapids: Eerdmans, 2011.

*Philo, Josephus, and the Testaments on Sexuality: Attitudes Towards Sexuality in the Writings of Philo, Josephus, and the Testaments of the Twelve Patriarchs.* Grand Rapids: Eerdmans, 2011.

*The New Testament on Sexuality.* Grand Rapids: Eerdmans, 2012.

## A brief summary volume draws all
## these together in overview:

*Making Sense of Sex: Attitudes towards Sexuality in Early Jewish and Christian Literature.* Grand Rapids: Eerdmans, 2013.

## My other related works include:

*Sexuality and Gender. Collected Essays.* WUNT 458. Tübingen: Mohr Siebeck, 2021.

*Sexuality in the New Testament.* Louisville: Westminster John Knox, 2010.

*The Septuagint, Sexuality, and the New Testament: Case Studies on the Impact of the LXX in Philo and the New Testament.* Grand Rapids: Eerdmans, 2004.

# Sources of Cited Translations
# of Ancient Texts

*The Bible. New Revised Standard Version containing the Old and New Testaments with the Apocryphal / Deuterocanonical Books.* New York: Oxford University Press, 1989.

Barclay, John M. G. *Against Apion.* Flavius Josephus: Translation and Commentary 10. Leiden: Brill, 2007.

Charlesworth, James H., ed. *The Old Testament Pseudepigrapha.* 2 vols. New York: Doubleday, 1983, 1985.

Colson F. H., G. H. Whittaker (and R. Marcus). *Philo in Ten Volumes (and Two Supplementary Volumes).* 12 vols. LCL. Cambridge: Harvard University Press, 1929–62.

Fitzmyer, Joseph A. *The Genesis Apocryphon of Qumran Cave 1 (1Q20): A Commentary.* 3rd ed. Biblica et Orientalia 18/B. Roma: Pontificio Istituto Biblico, 2004.

Hollander, Harm W., and Marinus de Jonge. *The Testaments of the Twelve Patriarchs: A Commentary.* SVTP 8. Leiden: Brill, 1985.

Nickelsburg, George W. E., and James C. VanderKam. *1 Enoch: A New Translation.* Minneapolis: Fortress, 2004.

Thackeray, H. St. John, Ralph Marcus, Allen Wikgren, and Louis H. Feldman. *Josephus.* LCL. 10 vols. Cambridge: Harvard University Press, 1926–1965.

Tov, Emanuel. *The Dead Sea Scrolls Electronic Library.* Leiden: Brill, 2006.

VanderKam, James C. *The Book of Jubilees.* 2 vols. CSCO 510–11. Louvain: Peeters, 1989.

Wilson, Walter T. *The Sentences of Pseudo-Phocylides.* CEJL. Berlin: de Gruyter, 2005.